5933   0588

ADDICTION

— AND —

OVERDOSE

CONFRONTING AN AMERICAN CRISIS

CONNIE GOLDSMITH

TWENTY-FIRST CENTURY BOOKS / MINNEAPOLIS

THIS BOOK IS DEDICATED TO MY SISTER, KERRI, WHO BATTLED
THE TWIN DEMONS OF DEPRESSION AND OPIOID USE FOR MANY YEARS.

Acknowledgments: The author especially wishes to thank Stephen Ahlert; Alisha Choquette;
Ellen Hopkins; Robert Kingwell, MD; Lauren Kramer; Brian and Donna Kull; and Leeann
Nielson, who shared their highly personal stories with me for this project, and the health-care
professionals social worker Sarah Gaskill; Earl Washburn, MD; and Tom Zimmerman, MD, who
shared their expertise.

Twenty-First Century Books
A division of Lerner Publishing Group, Inc.
241 First Avenue North
Minneapolis, MN 55401 USA

For reading levels and more information, look up this title at www.lernerbooks.com.

Main body text set in Adobe Garamond Pro 11/15
Typeface provided by Adobe Systems.

Library of Congress Cataloging-in-Publication Data

Names: Goldsmith, Connie, 1945– author.
Title: Addiction and overdose : confronting an American crisis / by Connie Goldsmith.
Description: Minneapolis : Twenty-First Century Books, [2017] | Includes bibliographical references
    and index.
Identifiers: LCCN 2016033031 (print) | LCCN 2016047771 (ebook) | ISBN 9781512409536 (lb : alk.
    paper) | ISBN 9781512448610 (eb pdf)
Subjects: LCSH: Drug addiction—United States—Juvenile literature. | Drug abuse—United States—
    Juvenile literature. | Medication abuse—United States—Juvenile literature. | Narcotics—
    Overdose—United States—Juvenile literature.
Classification: LCC RC564.3 .G65 2017 (print) | LCC RC564.3 (ebook) | DDC 362.290973—dc23

LC record available at https://lccn.loc.gov/2016033031

Manufactured in the United States of America
1-39550-21250-12/12/2016

CONTENTS

CHAPTER ONE
ADDICTION AND OVERDOSE IN AMERICA

Sunday, May 10, 2015, was a perfect Mother's Day for Donna Kull of Hillsborough, New Jersey. "The four of us had dinner together on the deck: my husband Brian, our son Adam, and his older sister," she says. "It was so pleasant—just what every mother hopes for—her grown children together and seemingly happy, everyone enjoying just being together for a meal."

Three days later, she was at her desk in the office where she worked as the secretary for a group of busy high school guidance counselors. "The call that changed our family's lives forever came into the office at 7:45 a.m.," she says. The mother of one of her son's friends was on the phone. "She was nervous, even a bit hysterical. It seemed like I had to pull the words out of her. 'Donna, these kids,' she said. 'I just don't know. He's gone.' 'Who?' I screamed. 'Who's gone?' 'Adam,' she said. 'He's dead at his apartment.' I yelled, 'NO! No, not Adam!'"

Kull's coworkers heard her anguished cry and gathered around her. "I said that my son had died and I needed to go. They

> "OVERDOSE DEATHS, PARTICULARLY FROM PRESCRIPTION DRUGS AND HEROIN, HAVE REACHED EPIDEMIC LEVELS."
>
> —Chuck Rosenberg, acting administrator, US Drug Enforcement Administration, 2015

wanted to take me, told me that I shouldn't drive, but I wouldn't listen. I don't remember my thoughts, I just knew that I had to leave and get to where Adam was. I grabbed my things and cursed God as I ran for my car. I drove as quickly as I could to Adam's apartment, about forty minutes away from my office." She knew her son used heroin, and she suspected an overdose had killed him.

LEFT BEHIND

Stories similar to Adam's happen far too often in the United States. Drug overdoses and deaths can happen anywhere: in the dark side streets and alleys of large inner cities; in small towns, rural areas, and suburbs; in poor as

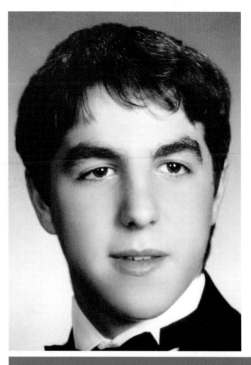

Adam Kull died in 2015 from an overdose of fentanyl-laced heroin. Fentanyl is an opioid prescription painkiller. He was one of nearly thirteen thousand Americans who died from a heroin overdose that year.

well as wealthy neighborhoods; and in small apartments and large homes. Its victims include teens and twenty-somethings with bright futures, high school and college athletes, blue- and white-collar workers, parents with young children, men and women, people of every race and identity, and older adults living with chronic pain. In 2015, the latest year for which the government has complete data, the states with the highest rates of overdose deaths in order were West Virginia, New Hampshire, Kentucky, Ohio, and Rhode Island.

Who dies of drug overdoses? A college athlete in Kentucky on Vicodin for a football injury. A suburban mother in New Hampshire taking Percocet for a broken ankle and Valium for anxiety. A farmworker in Ohio who was injured on the job. An unemployed coal miner in West Virginia using heroin because it's cheaper than the prescription painkillers he took for his back pain. Celebrities such as Prince and Michael Jackson, who both started taking prescription painkillers for legitimate reasons, became addicted, and eventually died from overdoses. And twenty-seven-year-old Adam Kull, a top wrestler and soccer player in high school who became addicted to a prescription medication for anxiety and then to heroin.

When Donna Kull arrived at her son's apartment, two police officers escorted her up the stairs. "I remember taking a very deep breath and looking into Adam's bedroom," she says. "He was lying on the floor with blood spilling from his mouth. The officers wouldn't let me go into the room, as it was still a crime scene." (Authorities consider the scene of a sudden, unexplained death to be a crime scene until the cause of death is determined and foul play is ruled out.) "From the doorway, I squatted down and looked at him, tears welling up in my eyes, shaking my head. I said, 'Why Adam! Why? I can't believe it.' I told him that I loved him, that I was proud of him, and then I said good-bye. Adam was on his way to the medical examiner's office in Newark [New Jersey] and I had to get home to tell my family." Like Donna Kull, the authorities suspected that Adam Kull had died of a drug overdose. The medical

Michael Jackson died in 2009 after his physician, Dr. Conrad Murray, injected him with the surgical anesthetic propofol, which Murray routinely used to help Jackson sleep. Jackson's years of addiction to Xanax and opioids likely contributed to his death. Jackson's addiction to prescription painkillers dated back to 1984, when he suffered serious scalp burns while filming a commercial.

examiner—a doctor who investigates suspicious deaths—would run blood tests to determine the specific cause of death.

Currently, drug overdoses are the leading cause of accidental death in the United States, surpassing deaths from auto accidents, suicides, and guns. Suicide and drugs are linked. While eight out of ten overdose deaths are accidents, one-third of the people who die from suicide are under the influence of drugs or alcohol at the time. Drug abuse can lead to depression, which in turn can lead to suicide by purposeful overdose.

Between 1999 and 2014, the number of deaths from auto accidents fell and deaths by gun violence rose only slightly. However, drug overdose deaths nearly tripled in that period and they keep rising. Just over 52,400 people in the United States died of drug overdoses in 2015, the latest year for which the US government has complete figures. These deaths affected tens of thousands of others as well. Most people who die from an overdose leave behind family members and friends who face a lifetime of grieving.

DRUG-INDUCED VERSUS OTHER DEATHS

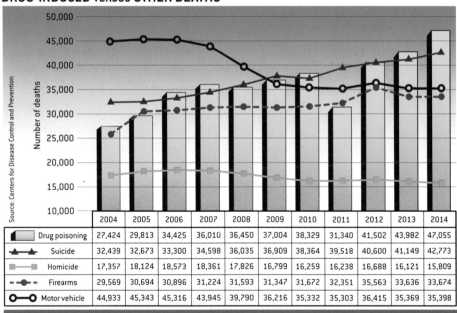

Source: Centers for Disease Control and Prevention

Number of deaths

	2004	2005	2006	2007	2008	2009	2010	2011	2012	2013	2014
Drug poisoning	27,424	29,813	34,425	36,010	36,450	37,004	38,329	31,340	41,502	43,982	47,055
Suicide	32,439	32,673	33,300	34,598	36,035	36,909	38,364	39,518	40,600	41,149	42,773
Homicide	17,357	18,124	18,573	18,361	17,826	16,799	16,259	16,238	16,688	16,121	15,809
Firearms	29,569	30,694	30,896	31,224	31,593	31,347	31,672	32,351	35,563	33,636	33,674
Motor vehicle	44,933	45,343	45,316	43,945	39,790	36,216	35,332	35,303	36,415	35,369	35,398

This graph, created by the Centers for Disease Control and Prevention, shows that drug-induced deaths in the United States are far outpacing the number of deaths from motor vehicle accidents, gun-related incidents, and other lethal events.

Adam Kull's mom keeps his Facebook page up so their family and friends can post messages. "When I post a message to Adam, it makes me feel like I'm talking to him," Donna Kull says. "I always hope his friends will comment on my posts." In January 2016, she posted, "We did get thru the holidays, but then we didn't have a choice—did we? Lots of distractions helped a bit, but there were moments. Now your birthday is nearing and that first big snowfall is sure to happen soon. I will remember how much you loved to see it, anxious to get on the mountain with your board. Love you." And in July 2016, "Well Adam, we were in Colorado last week to spread your ashes in this place that was so special to you. Your spirit will always be present in these beautiful mountains. Love you, Mom & Dad."

"Adam's sister is now an only child. She will never have a sibling to share family memories and holidays with. She will never know the joy and wonder of being an aunt. Hers is a long journey of healing."

—Brian Kull, 2016

Adam's friend James Weinberg wrote, "Miss you bro, I love you and wish I could be celebrating with you right now. Words can't describe the hole in my heart I have from you not being around to hang out with every day and to be celebrating your birthday with you right now."

Brian Kull says of his son, "How could a child raised with so many advantages fall prey to this disease [of addiction]? What could we have done differently? I wake each day and Adam is the first thing on my mind. I realize he's never walking through the door again, not next month or next year, and never is now an absolute. I constantly struggle to define my life knowing that I failed at the most important job I ever had—raising my child."

DEADLY DRUGS

When people hear the word *overdose*, they usually think about illegal drugs such as heroin, cocaine, and methamphetamine. And it's true that these illegal drugs kill many people. For example, heroin overdoses alone

DEATHS FROM DRUG OVERDOSING

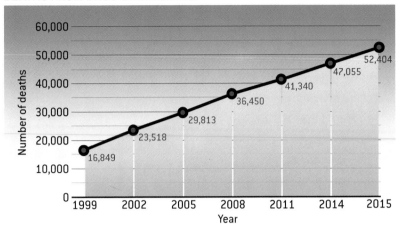

Source: Centers for Disease Control and Prevention

Deaths from drug overdoses in the United States more than tripled from 1999 to 2015. Americans overdose on opioids, over-the-counter drugs, stimulants, and sedatives.

killed nearly thirteen thousand people in 2015. Yet that same year about twenty-two thousand people died from overdoses of legal prescription painkillers (such as OxyContin and Vicodin) and illegally obtained or manufactured narcotics. Fatal overdoses from sedatives such as Valium, Ativan, and Xanax, prescribed for anxiety and insomnia, are on the increase as well, more than quadrupling since 2002.

These are the drugs most commonly involved in overdoses:

- **Over-the-counter (OTC) drugs** such as antihistamines and cough syrups. Even acetaminophen (a common ingredient in OTC pain relievers) can be deadly. In fact, acetaminophen is the most common cause of sudden liver failure in the United States.
- **Heroin** is an illegal and highly addictive drug that causes thousands of overdose deaths every year. Heroin is classified as a natural opiate and is derived from the opium poppy, which is widely grown in parts of Asia and the Middle East. Farmers cut

THE COST OF ADDICTION

The addiction and overdose crisis in the United States takes a terrible toll in human suffering. It also has a gigantic monetary cost. A Beth Israel Deaconess Medical Center and VA Boston Healthcare System study reported in 2016 that the cost of hospitalizations in the United States for opioid abuse and dependence nearly quadrupled to $15 billion between 2002 and 2012. Of that, $700 million paid for hospitalizations related to opioid-associated infections. These infections of the bone, heart, and brain come from sharing dirty needles. The average cost per hospitalization for the treatment of opioid abuse was $28,000. Treatment for an infection associated with opioid abuse was more than $107,000.

Dr. Shoshana Herzig, coauthor of the study, said, "The . . . consequences of opioid abuse and dependence, including serious infection, are severe—for individual patients and their loved ones, caregivers, hospital systems, and the federal government [the most common payer for opioid-associated hospitalizations]."

into the seedpod of the poppy to release the thick, milky opium sap. Once exposed to the air, the sap turns into a brownish-black, gumlike substance. Natural opiates include morphine, heroin, and codeine.

- **Prescription painkillers** are classified as opioids, and many people use them for severe pain. Opioids are synthetic forms of opiates, manufactured in legitimate laboratories for medical use and sometimes in illegal laboratories for recreational use. Opioids differ from opiates in their chemical structure, although they have similar effects on the human brain and body as do natural opiates. Like opiates, opioids can be extremely addictive. So they are often abused and cause a large number of nonlethal overdoses as well as overdose deaths. Opioids include the generic medications hydrocodone, oxycodone, hydromorphone, and fentanyl. The brand names are OxyContin, Percocet, Percodan, Vicodin, Demerol, Roxanol, Opana, Zohydro, and many others. The terms *opiate* and *opioid* are often used interchangeably in the media, with *opioid* the most common.

- **Methamphetamine** is an illegal and highly addictive synthetic stimulant. Unrelated to opioids or opiates, it can still cause overdose deaths.
- **Cocaine** is another illegal and highly addictive stimulant, also unrelated to opioids or opiates. Cocaine comes from the leaves of the South American coca plant.
- **Sedatives** are the generic name for a class of drugs called benzodiazepines (such as Valium and Xanax). Doctors prescribe benzodiazepines and antidepressants such as Zoloft, Prozac, and Cymbalta much more often than opioid painkillers. Overdose deaths in the United States from these medications are also on the rise.
- **Taking a combination of drugs and alcohol** is extremely dangerous and more likely to lead to death than using either alone.

Doctors and law enforcement officials categorize prescription painkillers and heroin as narcotics. While people may call any illegal drug a narcotic, medical and legal experts most often use the word for drugs related to the opioid family. The word *narcotic* comes from a Greek word meaning "to make numb," and that's just what these drugs do. When used in moderation, prescription painkillers are very effective at relieving pain and promoting sleep. When used in excess, these drugs can kill.

Along with heroin, prescription painkillers can cause euphoria, or a high, an extreme sense of well-being that users often wish to experience over and over. The high comes from the way the drugs change the chemistry in the brain. However, when taken in excess, narcotics depress the brain's respiratory center. The lungs stop working because they are no longer getting signals from the brain to breathe. When the lungs stop functioning, the heart goes into cardiac arrest and stops beating because the lungs are no longer providing it with oxygen. Without medical intervention, death follows quickly.

In Adam Kull's case, the police initially believed that he had died of a heroin overdose. But toxicology reports—tests on blood, urine, and bodily tissues—later showed that he had unknowingly injected fentanyl-laced heroin. Fentanyl is an opioid prescription painkiller that's thirty to fifty times more potent than heroin. Doctors prescribe it most often to people with severe pain from cancer and following major surgery. Surgeons may use it during surgery as part of anesthesia. While no one can be sure how Adam got access to fentanyl, an illegal drug that labs and dealers

SAVE A LIFE

Take these steps to help save people who may be overdosing:

- Stay with them and keep talking. Reassure them and try to make them talk to you.

- If they are unconscious, turn them to the side. This position helps protect the airway and prevents inhaling stomach contents in case of vomiting.

- Call 911 and follow the operator's instructions until emergency medical personnel arrive.

- Do not leave the victim alone. Stay until help arrives.

- Ask if you should ride in the ambulance. The paramedics or emergency room doctor may have questions about the overdose victim. Ask if you should notify the victim's family or another appropriate person about the overdose. Often that responsibility belongs to the attending physician or other emergency room staff.

commonly mix into heroin and prescription painkillers to provide a stronger high.

The Atlanta-based Centers for Disease Control and Prevention (CDC)—the US government agency charged with promoting the health and safety of Americans—reports a startling spike in fentanyl-related overdose deaths. Mixing illegally manufactured fentanyl with heroin significantly increases its potency, and users can therefore easily overdose. "Drug incidents and overdoses related to fentanyl are occurring at an alarming rate throughout the United States and represent a significant threat to public health and safety," Michele Leonhart of the US Drug Enforcement Administration (DEA) said in 2015. Legal and illegally manufactured Fentanyl are included in the CDC's 2015 data regarding death by opioid overdose.

Adam Kull didn't know that the heroin he injected contained fentanyl. He never stood a chance. He died almost instantly.

BY THE NUMBERS

» More than fifty-two thousand people died of drug overdoses in the United States in 2015.

» Heroin caused nearly thirteen thousand of those deaths.

» Heroin laced with synthetic fentanyl is thirty to fifty times more potent—and, therefore, more dangerous—than straight heroin.

CHAPTER TWO
THE POWER OF ADDICTION

Ellen Hopkins, best-selling author of twelve young adult novels, knows all too well about addiction and the power it has to control and ruin lives. "I've built a career that many writers envy, and yet I'm rarely able to truly relax. I've forgotten in too many ways, what 'fun' is. Not because of what I do, but because of what brought me here."

She says, "My first young adult novel, *Crank*, was inspired by a very real story of addiction, one that shattered our family twenty-one years ago, and continues to rattle our lives today. It's the story of my daughter Cristal, an upper-middle class, straight-A kid, a girl with the potential of making huge contributions to the world. Instead, she chose to experiment with methamphetamine. That choice, at age seventeen, destroyed her dreams and led to her implosion. She has lied to us.

> "ADDICTION CAN BECOME MORE IMPORTANT THAN THE NEED TO EAT OR SLEEP. THE URGE TO GET AND USE THE DRUG CAN FILL EVERY MOMENT OF A PERSON'S LIFE. THE ADDICTION REPLACES ALL THE THINGS THE PERSON USED TO ENJOY."
>
> —National Institute on Drug Abuse, 2016

Stolen from us. Threatened us. Tried to blackmail us. Anything for another hit."

Thousands of young people know about Cristal and her addiction because Hopkins has been remarkably open about sharing those experiences with her teen readers. "I wanted to be clear that the *Crank* trilogy was rooted in fact so that no one could say, 'This could never happen.' It did happen, and it is my fervent hope that reading these books will keep other young people from veering down that path."

Hopkins says recovery is possible for many people, but for her daughter, addiction controls her life. "Over the

Best-selling author Ellen Hopkins has written about her daughter's downward spiral as a result of addiction to methamphetamines. She describes the devastation in a trilogy of YA novels known as the *Crank* trilogy. The three novels include the first, *Crank*, followed by *Glass* and *Fallout*.

past two decades, Cristal has maintained periods of sober living, all of which ended with eventual relapses. She has suffered through rehab, endured counseling, and worked programs like Alcoholics Anonymous and Narcotics Anonymous, sometimes celebrating multiple years clean before the inevitable backslide."

Hopkins says, "It would be easy to say it's her life, and she can do with it as she pleases. But no one's life is completely their own. Cristal has had seven children, with seven different fathers. Only the youngest is in her care. My husband and I adopted the first, who is nineteen. The second and third (ages fifteen and thirteen) have been with their paternal aunts since my daughter went to prison in 2002. The next three (now eleven, seven and five) came to live with me under devastating circumstances three years ago. One suffers from post-traumatic stress caused by the trauma [related to his mother's addiction] he experienced in his early childhood. All remember their mother; none want to return to her."

Hopkins says, "My author's note in *Crank* says, 'It's hard to watch someone you love fall so deeply under the spell of a substance that turns him or her into a stranger. Someone you don't even want to know.' The truth is it's more than hard—it's heart wrenching. Today, my daughter has physical and mental health issues, all attributable to meth. She will never be one hundred percent okay. Neither will I and neither will her children, because of a choice she made long before she was mature enough to fully understand the consequences."

THE BRAIN'S NATURAL HIGH

Why can addiction take over and control a life as it did with Cristal? The answer lies in the brain. The adult human brain weighs about 3 pounds (1.4 kilograms) and contains an estimated two hundred billion neurons (nerve cells), each connected to thousands of other neurons. These neurons form complex communication pathways that deliver messages to and from different areas of the brain, the spinal cord, and all the nerves in the body. These messages allow us to move, to think and dream, and to feel love and sadness. They allow us to respond to pleasant experiences such as a hug from a friend and to unpleasant experiences such as a burned finger. The messages tell the heart to beat and the lungs to breathe.

The brain is all about communication among its neurons. Inside the brain, dendrites bring information *to* a neuron, while axons take information *away* from a neuron. In both cases, this information is transmitted as electrical impulses. But axons and dendrites don't quite meet. Instead, a miniscule gap called the synapse separates them. The electrical impulse cannot jump across the synapse to deliver its message. So how does the massive flow of information get passed on from the axon of one neuron to the dendrite of another?

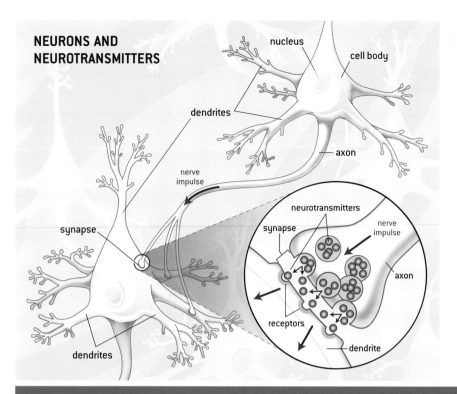

NEURONS AND NEUROTRANSMITTERS

nucleus

cell body

dendrites

axon

nerve impulse

synapse

neurotransmitters

synapse

nerve impulse

axon

receptors

dendrite

dendrites

Information moves through the brain as electrical impulses among neurons. Dendrites bring information to a neuron. Axons carry information away. The gap between dendrites and axons is called a synapse, or synaptic gap. Chemicals called neurotransmitters relay the message across the synapse.

The ends of axons nearest the synapse contain tiny packets of chemicals called neurotransmitters. When the axons release the neurotransmitters, the chemicals carry the message across the synapse to receptors on the dendrite. Scientists believe the brain has up to one hundred different neurotransmitters. Once across the synapse, each type of neurotransmitter fits into only one type of receptor—similar to a key fitting into a lock.

Four neurotransmitters in the brain provide most of the chemicals that naturally make us feel good.

1. **Dopamine** helps us focus and is responsible for drive and ambition. When we achieve a goal, dopamine gives us a surge of pleasure to reinforce the act and encourage us to repeat it.

2. **Endorphins** are released when we feel pain or stress. They help to decrease pain, anxiety, and depression. Exercise, laughter, and other pleasant activities can increase endorphins.
3. **Serotonin** flows through the brain when you feel valued and that you belong.
4. **Oxytocin**—sometimes called the cuddle hormone—creates intimacy and trust and builds healthy relationships.

Humans, as well as other animals, naturally want to do the things that make them feel better. Spending time with friends, laughing at a joke, or eating a chocolate chip cookie makes us happy. The pleasure we experience is a positive reinforcement—an incentive to repeat those activities. The brain's reward pathways—circuits of neurons that travel to several areas deep within the brain—are responsible for driving our feelings of motivation, reward, and behavior. By giving us a jolt of pleasure, the reward pathways work to ensure that we will repeat behaviors such as eating, which are necessary for survival. If you are hungry and a friend gives you nachos, you remember that when you eat, you no longer feel hungry. You eat the nachos. Instead of the uncomfortable feeling of hunger, you experience the pleasure of eating. The reward pathways have done their job.

Scientists at Johns Hopkins University in Baltimore, Maryland, were studying drug addiction and the human brain in 1972 when they made a surprising discovery. They found that certain neurons in the brain have specific receptor sites for opiates such as heroin, codeine, and morphine. The researchers called the sites opioid receptors. Once inside the brain, all opiates convert to morphine, which binds directly with the opioid receptors.

The discovery raised an important question: Why does the human brain contain receptors for morphine? Morphine comes from the sap of the opium poppy. Scientists were certain that human brains did not evolve to contain receptors for morphine. The scientists were convinced these receptors must have another function—a natural function that had nothing to do with dangerously addictive drugs.

Three independent groups of scientists working in the United States, Scotland, and Sweden found the answer in 1973. They discovered that the brain produces its own version of morphine. They called the group of naturally produced brain chemicals endorphins, short for endogenous (internally produced) morphine, even though endorphins are not actually morphine. Endorphins attach to the opioid receptors just like morphine does.

THE ADDICTED BRAIN

The discovery of opioid receptors and endorphins opened the door to understanding addiction. Endorphins are the body's natural pain-relieving chemicals. If you sprain your ankle, the brain knows all about it. Nerve impulses travel from the ankle to the spinal cord and then to the brain to say, "Ouch! This hurts." That triggers the brain to release endorphins, which bind to the opioid receptors to reduce the perception of pain and stress. Your ankle is still red and swollen, but your brain tells you it doesn't hurt quite as much as it did at first. Endorphins not only block pain, but they also produce pleasurable feelings. Vigorous exercise such as a run or an energetic workout at the gym causes the brain to release endorphins. They may produce a runner's high, a feeling of happiness and

OPIOID RECEPTORS

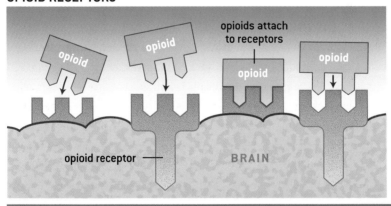

Some neurons in the brain have specific receptor sites for opiates. These sites are called opioid receptors. When opioids bind with the receptor, the body releases dopamine, which creates a sense of well-being, relaxation, pleasure, and freedom from pain.

well-being that can encourage people to continue their run or workout.

Once endorphins bind with the opioid receptors, they signal the brain to release dopamine, which produces pleasure and relaxation. Dopamine and endorphins are the neurotransmitters that are most affected by addiction. The brain normally maintains just the right amounts of those neurotransmitters to keep us feeling well. Neurons along the reward pathways release endorphins in response to pain and stress. Endorphins bind to opioid receptors and signal the brain to release dopamine. The dopamine momentarily binds to dopamine receptors before returning to the neuron that released it. And after endorphins bind with opioid receptors and stimulate dopamine release, the brain's enzymes (chemical substances that perform specific functions in the body) destroy them. In the absence of addictive drugs, the brain constantly recycles dopamine and endorphins to maintain stable amounts of these neurotransmitters in the brain.

People crave the pleasure that comes with stimulating the brain's reward centers. For some people, that may mean eating ice cream or taking a run in the park. For others, it means using illegal drugs or abusing prescription painkillers. When ingested or injected, prescription and illegal opioids result in less pain and increased pleasure and relaxation. Dr. William Stanley, medical director of a rehabilitation center, says, "Clients have described the high [of an opioid drug] as imagining your happiest moment and multiplying it by 5, 10, 15." The feelings of pleasure, pain relief, and euphoria from using opioids become their own reward. The reward is difficult, then eventually nearly impossible, to resist.

Scientists discovered that the brain's reward system is so strong that lab rats in a heroin experiment will repeatedly press a lever to inject themselves with the drug simply because it makes them feel good. Rats display the same behavior whether the heroin is injected into a blood vessel in the body (as a human user would do) or into the brain. The rat's drive to obtain heroin is so powerful that it continues to self-administer heroin even when it receives a painful electrical shock from the heroin-releasing lever.

Addictive drugs such as heroin inhibit the recycling of dopamine and

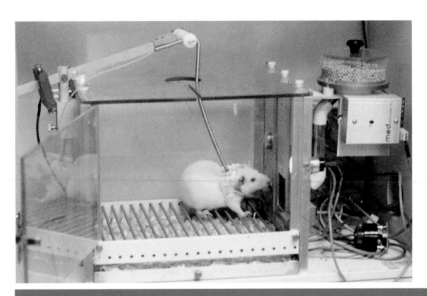

Addiction to opioids is so strong that humans and lab rats, such as this one in a heroin experiment, typically continue to use the drugs even if consequences are painful or otherwise harmful.

endorphins. Extremely high levels of these neurotransmitters remain in the brain, stimulating it, fooling it, forcing it to send false messages. Many drugs, including alcohol, nicotine, cocaine, opioids, and methamphetamine, increase dopamine in the brain. When a person regularly uses these substances, the brain produces so much dopamine that it cannot reabsorb it quickly enough. Instead, this flood of dopamine disrupts the way neurons in the brain send, receive, and process information by overstimulating the reward centers of the brain. Whether ingested, injected, or snorted, opioids go directly to the opioid receptor sites and sit there. They encourage other parts of the brain to release large amounts of dopamine. Before long, the brain forgets how to produce its own dopamine, instead depending on opioid drugs to stimulate its production. This is a driving force in addiction.

Opioid receptors occur in many parts of the brain. Once inside the body, some opioids bind to receptors that reduce pain perception. Opioids that bind to receptors in deeper parts of the brain may result in a slower heart rate and depressed breathing—the primary cause of opioid overdose deaths. With continued use of opioid drugs, the body's production of natural endorphins and dopamine decline. This causes many of the painful symptoms of opioid withdrawal (severe symptoms that include agitation and anxiety, nausea and vomiting, abdominal pain and muscle aches) when a person stops taking an addictive drug.

Opioids are far more powerful than the body's own pain relievers— endorphins—and they resist being destroyed by enzymes. So they stay in the body much longer than endorphins and prolong pain relief and relaxation. Doctors prescribe opioids after surgery or serious injuries for the long-term pain relief. When patients use opioid medications as directed, they seldom experience strong feelings of euphoria. Instead, patients feel less pain, which aids in faster recovery.

WHAT IS ADDICTION?

Many people cannot understand how or why someone would take drugs or how addiction happens. Those people may believe that drug abusers lack willpower or morals and that they could simply stop taking drugs if they really wanted to. While the initial decision to take drugs for nonmedical reasons is voluntary, many people are unable to stop—even when they want to—once addiction takes over. Brain-imaging studies from drug addicts show physical changes in parts of the brain where judgment, decision making, learning, memory, and self-control take place. Scientists believe these changes permanently affect how the brain works and may help explain the compulsive and destructive behaviors of an addicted person.

What is it like to be addicted? Journalist David Muir followed several heroin addicts in a small New Hampshire town for a 2016 ABC television special titled *Breaking Point: Heroin in America*. Aaron Smith, a twenty-two-year-old husband and father, had been using heroin for one year. "It snowballed really quickly, to the point where I get up every day and my number one task is heroin," he told Muir. Smith reported stealing from his family to support his habit. "Family members that you once loved, all they are to you is a money sign. [Addiction] brings you to something lower than a human being." He used heroin just a few hours before admission to a rehab program. At that point, he said, "Right now I just want to get high even more. I know it's destroyed my life, but right now I just want to get high." Smith stayed in rehab for three days before checking himself out. Eight days later, he died of a heroin overdose.

Kimberly Bussey became addicted to prescription painkillers in her mid-twenties after she received them while hospitalized following a miscarriage. She said, "The medications don't just take away the pain, they make you feel really, really good." When she couldn't afford the pills any longer, she turned to heroin, which she could purchase cheaply on the street. Within a year, addiction took over her life. She could no longer care for her young son and lost custody of him. She lost her job. She also lost her car and her house because she used her money to buy drugs instead of paying her bills.

Twenty-one-year-old Savannah quickly fell into heroin addiction as well. "One time is all it took [for me] and within a month I was shooting up. I was so oblivious and high all the time that I didn't even realize I was five months pregnant." She managed to get help and was clean for a few months after the birth of her child. When her husband went to jail for drug-related crimes, the family fell apart and she began using again. Like Bussey, she lost custody of her child.

Aaron Smith, Kimberly Bussey, and Savannah are examples of people who are addicted to drugs. Several terms—drug dependence, drug tolerance, and drug addiction—describe the continuum of drug use and abuse.

Drug dependence may occur in people using prescription opioids for chronic pain over a long period of time. Typically, people using prescription opioids for legitimate medical reasons do not experience—nor do they seek—the high that may come with the abuse of legal opioids such as oxycodone. Opioids relieve most of their pain, and they can go on with their lives. Even so, patients taking opioids get used to receiving regular doses of the medication and can only function normally while taking it.

People who use opioids for nonmedical purposes may also experience drug dependence. While the drugs may not destroy their lives, these people must continue to take the drugs to avoid withdrawal.

Drug tolerance occurs when the body adapts to or gets used to a particular medication or drug, such as prescription painkillers or heroin. Then the drug does little to relieve pain or to achieve the desired high. The person must take increasingly larger amounts of the drug to achieve the same effect. Some people switch to another drug instead. Neither drug dependence nor drug tolerance is the same as addiction, although both have the potential to lead to addiction.

Drug addiction drastically changes behavior as well as the brain itself. (Some experts use the term *substance use disorder* instead of *addiction*.) The National Council on Alcoholism and Drug Dependence says, "Addiction is a chronic, often relapsing [period of getting worse after getting better] brain disease that causes compulsive drug seeking and use, despite harmful consequences to the addicted individual and to those around him or her. . . . The brain changes that occur over time challenge an addicted person's self-control and hamper his or her ability to resist intense impulses to take drugs." The powerful craving for the pleasurable high that the drug brings and the fear of withdrawal are what keeps addicts using drugs.

The website of *Psychology Today*, a respected medical magazine, defines addiction as, "a condition that results when a person ingests a substance [for example, opioids, heroin, or methamphetamine] . . . that can be pleasurable, but the continued use. . . of which becomes compulsive and interferes with ordinary life responsibilities, such as work, relationships, or health. Users may not be aware that their behavior is out of control and causing problems for themselves and others."

The common theme in these definitions is that people addicted to drugs lose control of their behavior and of their lives. They continue to hunt for drugs and to use them, knowing that the drugs are likely to harm themselves and others around them. The addict is unable to reduce or give up the drugs even though they interfere with major life obligations, damage personal relationships, and lead to spending a great deal of time and money to procure the drugs. The euphoria and relaxation opioids produce may be so compelling and enjoyable for some people that they will do nearly anything to experience those feelings again and again. According to the American Society of Addiction Medicine, of the 21.5 million Americans aged twelve or older who had a substance abuse disorder in 2014, 1.9 million abused prescription painkillers, while well over half a million abused heroin.

WHO GETS ADDICTED?

According to the NIDA (National Institute on Drug Abuse), no one factor can predict whether a person will become addicted to drugs. The risk for any one person is influenced by elements such as individual biology, social environment, and age. The more risk factors in people's lives, the more likely they are to become addicted. The risk factors include these:

- *Biology:* According to the National Council on Alcoholism and Drug Dependence, studies show that genetics make up one-half of a person's susceptibility to drug or alcohol addiction.
- *Environment:* Socioeconomic status, peer pressure, gender, mental health issues, family support or lack of support, stress, physical abuse or sexual abuse or both and other trauma, and general quality of life issues are environmental factors that may contribute to risks for becoming addicted. One risk factor alone seldom leads to addiction. The more risk factors in a person's life, the greater the risk of addiction.
- *Development:* Taking drugs can lead to addiction at any age. However, the earlier people start using drugs, the more likely they are to progress to abuse and addiction. Teen brains are amazing works in progress. Yet regions of the brain that manage executive functions such as decision making, judgment, and self-control are not fully developed until about the age of

twenty-five. Teens and young adults may be especially prone to risk-taking behaviors that lead to addiction, including using illegal drugs. Dr. Daniel J. Siegel, addiction specialist and brain researcher, says "Dopamine levels at baseline are lower and the dopamine release amounts are higher [in adolescents]. . . . What this helps explain is some of the boredom of adolescents and the drive toward doing [new] things." A new experience, such as trying an addictive drug results in higher levels of dopamine in adolescents than in adults. "And that can explain the risk-taking behavior," Siegel said.

Many people who are addicted to drugs also live with a mental illness, according to the NIDA. People with mental health challenges—such as depression, anxiety, or bipolar disorder (in which a person alternates between depressive and manic behaviors)—are about twice as likely to also suffer from a substance use disorder as are people without mental illnesses. Experts use the term *dual diagnosis* to describe people living with both mental illness and substance abuse. Experts point out that mental illness does not necessarily cause substance abuse nor does using drugs lead to mental illness. However, using drugs may worsen the symptoms of an existing mental illness. And mental illness may lead a person to self-medicate with drugs in an attempt to manage their moods or behavior. The NIDA says that it's likely that underlying factors such as genetic vulnerabilities and exposure to stress and trauma at an early age cause both substance abuse and mental illness.

SAYING NO

The American Society of Addiction Medicine says that most teens who abuse prescription painkillers receive them from friends or relatives who are unaware of the dangers of using opioid drugs for nonmedical use. According to the NIDA, most drug use starts in the teen years, sometimes as early as twelve or thirteen years old. More people start using illegal drugs between the ages of sixteen and seventeen than at any other age. Certain transitional periods in a teen's life, such as moving, changing schools, and difficult family problems such as divorce or death may increase the risk of teens trying drugs. Even so, most young people reject drugs.

Lucy is seventeen years old and in the eleventh grade. "Kids talk about marijuana, and vape pens are very common at my school. I've never been asked to buy or use any drugs, but I believe people who want drugs can go out and find someone to supply them. I'm very focused on school, so I dislike any type of distraction. I have two younger brothers who I am a role model for, and my friends are interested in other, more productive ways to pass the time. Remember, nobody will freak out if you say no when offered drugs. Not participating in something illegal doesn't make you less cool, less popular, or less attractive."

Nate is sixteen years old and in the tenth grade. "Kids at my school talk about all kinds of stuff, from parties to smoking pot after class. I often see kids smoking weed behind buildings. Every few weeks, one of my classmates is stoned in class—not always the same kid. Once, in the locker room, a kid offered me a weed brownie, and another time a teammate had a water bottle filled with alcohol. Doing drugs is stupid and there could be so many consequences."

A combination of many factors can lead to addiction. These include a genetic predisposition to addiction, lack of emotional support in life, abuse, peer pressure to take drugs, depression or other mental health challenges, and dangerous risk-taking behaviors.

THE DRUG DANGER ZONE

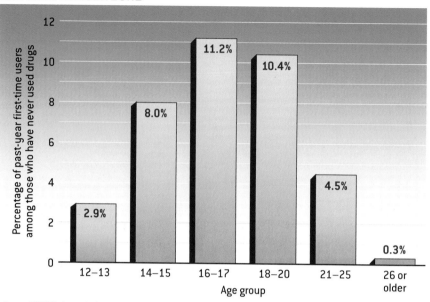

Source: SAMHSA, Center for Behavioral Health Statistics and Quality, National Survey on Drug Use and Health, 2011 and 2012

This chart illustrates that most illegal drug use starts between the ages of sixteen and seventeen. As a person matures, the likelihood of trying an illegal drug lessens dramatically.

Megan is fifteen years old and in the tenth grade. "My group of friends jokes about drugs. We know we're never going to take them because of the negative effects. No one ever offered drugs to me, but I'd refuse if they did. I don't want to mess up my life by making a stupid decision. I play sports and don't want to ruin my high school sports career. I plan on going to college and don't want to spoil my chances of getting accepted to where I want to go." Megan wants to tell other teens: "Don't do drugs. If you have hopes of being successful in life, taking drugs is going to smash your dreams. You were given a brain for a reason—use it!"

Alexandra is sixteen years old and in the eleventh grade. "Kids at my school talk about weed, but nobody offers to give me any because they know I don't do drugs. I just don't hang out with that crowd. I really don't want to do illegal drugs, even though the kids I know who do drugs are okay, pretty chill. I'm involved in acting and chorus and don't have the time or energy for drugs." Alexandra says to other teens, "Don't do drugs because they're bad for you!"

A PREVENTABLE DISEASE

Drug addiction is a preventable disease. Learn everything you can about prescription narcotics and illegal drugs, their dangerous side effects, and how easily they can ruin lives and lead to deadly overdoses. Follow your doctor's directions exactly if you receive a prescription painkiller. Cravings can begin for some people with the first dose of an opioid drug whether illegal or prescribed. Continuing to take the substance greatly increases the risk of addiction. Turn to trusted adults or your doctor for help if you experience these cravings or if you are being pressured to try drugs.

TIPS FOR TEENS

The National Council on Alcoholism and Drug Dependence offers tips to teens to help prevent alcohol and drug problems. Among them are these points:

1. Say no. Make your own decisions. Don't let "everybody is doing it" influence you.

2. Stick with your friends who don't use drugs, and avoid hanging out with those who do.

3. Connect with your parents and trusted adults. Their experience may guide you.

4. Be a role model and set a good example for your siblings and other kids.

5. Enjoy life and do what you love. There really is no time to waste on drugs.

6. Get help if you or someone you know is in trouble with drugs. Don't wait.

Saying no isn't always easy, but you can do it. Brian Kull, who lost his son Adam to drugs, wants teens to know this: "It's important to understand the fragility of life, the fine line that separates success from failure, happiness from despair, inner peace from turmoil, and self-determination from dependency. Once a teen begins to use drugs, some will lose control of their lives. History is littered with highly successful athletes, musicians, movie stars, bankers, lawyers, doctors, and folks in all walks of life who became powerless under the influence of drugs. The only sure path is to avoid drugs entirely."

BY THE NUMBERS

» About 1.9 million Americans abuse prescription painkillers every year.

» The brains of teens and young adults are not fully mature until the age of twenty-five.

» More people begin taking drugs between the ages of sixteen and seventeen than any other age group.

CHAPTER THREE
FACES OF ADDICTION

"The disease of addiction can grab hold of anyone and destroy your life in an instant," says twenty-five-year-old Stephen Ahlert of Providence, Rhode Island. "For me, it all stems back to the day when I tried drugs for the first time. I knew I shouldn't have done it; I was scared and really didn't want to, but I did it anyway because everyone else was doing it. That moment was the beginning of a war that I fight every day."

Up until the ninth grade, Stephen lived a charmed life. His parents encouraged him to work hard at school and sports. He was an honor student and a top athlete at a small private school where drugs were not commonly used. When he entered a large public high school, "Life as I knew it changed. I was suddenly exposed to sex, drugs, and alcohol." Until then, Stephen had dreamed of becoming an attorney or a teacher when he grew up. Instead, he became a drug dealer at sixteen.

"I was drinking and smoking weed, but these were expensive habits, so I started selling weed to pay for my own habit. All of a sudden, I had plenty of money, nice clothes, and was one of the 'cool kids' who was always partying. Selling drugs turned me from a drug

"YOU CAN DRAW A STRAIGHT LINE FROM PHARMACEUTICAL OPIATES TO SHOOTING HEROIN."

—Mark Nomady, former agent with the US Drug Enforcement Administration, 2016

Addiction can harm just about anyone, regardless of race, gender, class, or other identity factor. However, studies are showing that the current opioid overdose epidemic is impacting white Americans more than other groups. White Americans are twice as likely to die from a drug overdose as African Americans and four times more likely than Hispanics.

dealer into a drug addict. Next, I started using cocaine. Then I was hanging out with a crowd who popped Vicodin like it was candy. I did something I vowed I would never do; I crushed and snorted a Percocet. This was the moment when I lost myself."

By the time he finished high school, his physical tolerance for opioids had grown. "I started popping handfuls of Vicodin, then when that wasn't enough, I started snorting them." Ahlert went from being a drug dealer to owing $40,000 to his own dealer. When the dealer cut off his drug supply, Ahlert sold everything he owned—two cars, a motorcycle, a television, and his furniture—to pay for drugs. Then he switched to heroin because it cost so much less than prescription painkillers.

"During the last months of my heroin use, I was beyond being out of control. I was coming into contact with the police literally every other day for theft, DUI [driving under the influence], and driving without a license. I didn't care about anything but heroin. I really thought I was invincible. Then one day, a blessing in disguise happened—I went to jail. Sitting there in the cell, sick from withdrawal, I finally realized I needed serious professional help." By then Ahlert had lost everything. "I had no job, no home, no car, no money, and my family relationships were destroyed, all because I picked heroin over everything else. It became a toxic cycle for me because I was always surrounded by drug use and was willing and wanting to try anything."

After he got out of jail, he entered a drug treatment program and succeeded in kicking his heroin habit. "I use the life I lived and all the things I lost as my fuel and motivation to stay clean and to work towards the goals and aspirations that I once lost sight of." Ahlert is twenty-five years old and working toward a degree in substance abuse counseling. "I hope to start a career as a counselor and coach. It's a constant battle with my disease of addiction, but I fight every day and thank God that I'm winning the war, one day at a time."

PRESCRIPTION ADDICTION

Ahlert got clean and survived. Many people don't. According to the CDC, deaths from opioid drug overdoses in both women and men are at an all-time high and are still climbing. "The increasing number of deaths from opioid overdose is alarming," CDC director Dr. Tom Frieden said. "The opioid epidemic is devastating American families and communities." According to the National Institutes of Health, the nonmedical use of prescription painkillers has doubled since 2001, with about ten million Americans reporting they abused or misused opioid painkillers between 2012 and 2013 alone.

Most Americans know about and are concerned about opioid abuse and addiction. Yet even with this knowledge, more than one in four has taken prescription painkillers over the past year, according to a recent study published by the journal *Addiction*. Seven out of ten Americans have taken prescription painkillers in their lifetime, and more than 17 percent reported using these medications even though a doctor had not prescribed them. And every day, about sixty-two Americans die from an opioid overdose, including prescription painkillers, and other legal and illegal opioid drugs.

A *National Geographic* article in 2014 about heroin describes a heroin overdose this way:

> A heroin overdose happens because use of the drug alters the neurons within every addict's brain—but the alterations occur in different parts of the brain at varying rates of speed. The pleasure center, increasingly hard to satisfy, is screaming 'More!' But primitive centers that control breathing and heart rate are not building up tolerance at the same pace and are whispering 'Enough.'

The pleasure center wins, the addict takes too much of the drug, and the primitive centers that control breathing and heart rate stop working. Death soon follows. The same thing happens with a prescription painkiller overdose.

Dr. Andrew Kolodny is an expert in addiction medicine, the executive director of Physicians for Responsible Opioid Prescribing, and the chief medical officer of Phoenix House, a nonprofit addiction treatment organization with rehab facilities in several states. "When we talk about opioid painkillers, we are essentially talking about heroin pills," he says. "There is very good evidence that the vast majority of the overdose deaths that we're experiencing are not occurring in recreational drug users. They're occurring in people who develop opioid addiction. Some people develop opioid addiction through recreational and nonmedical use, but many people are suffering from this condition because they developed it taking pills exactly the way the doctor . . . prescribed."

In a 2015 feature article in *Time*, the magazine noted that "[opioids are] the most powerful painkillers ever invented. And they're creating the worst addiction crisis America has ever seen." The article pointed out that the crisis often begins in doctors' offices where ordinary people seek help for pain. "Around the nation, doctors so frequently prescribe the drugs known as opioids for chronic pain . . . that there are enough pills prescribed every year to keep every American adult medicated around the clock for a month."

If your doctor gives you a prescription for Percodan for your sprained ankle, it must be safe, right? Or if your dentist prescribes a bottle of Vicodin after pulling a wisdom tooth, it's got to be okay because you're in pain, correct? Your doctor and dentist know what they're doing, don't they? Not necessarily. Kolodny asked, "Would a dentist really give a teenager 30 Vicodins after a wisdom tooth extraction if the dentist realized the Vicodins were essentially heroin pills?"

Many experts believe that doctors, especially primary care physicians, don't have enough training in prescribing opioid medications. "The biggest part of the problem," Kolodny said, "is the well-meaning doctors and dentists who underestimate how addictive these pills are and overestimate how effective they are." In fact, doctors prescribe opioid painkillers for one-fifth of the patients who complain of pain not caused by cancer.

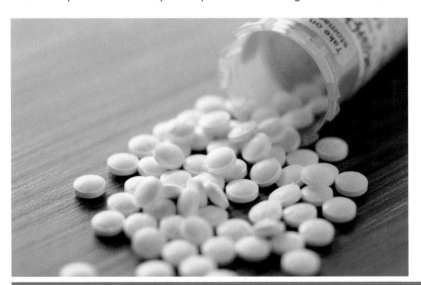

Many Americans have become addicted to opioids through legitimate prescriptions from their doctors. Yet in some cases, physicians were prescribing painkillers for conditions that did not require such intensive drug therapy.

Michael Beltzer is a thirty-year-old former elected member of the Bronx Community Board 9. This local government unit of New York City works to improve the quality of life for its residents. Beltzer knows all about prescription painkillers and how easy it is to get addicted. A few years ago, he developed severe neck pain, and his doctor prescribed oxycodone. Beltzer soon became dependent on the painkiller and even exaggerated his pain so the doctor would continue to prescribe the medication. He learned how to crush the tablets and snort the white powder to maximize his high. He began each morning by snorting oxycodone, a daily routine that lasted five years.

Beltzer's addiction to prescription painkillers became the focus of his life. Besides his morning fix, Michael needed one or two tablets to make it through an eight-hour workday. He worried he would run out of pills. So he convinced two doctors to give him separate prescriptions for a total of 720 oxycodone pills per month. His performance at work was so poor that he lost his job. Then he went cold turkey—immediately and completely stopping his drug use—and went through a painful withdrawal. (This method can be dangerous because potential complications of withdrawal can be severe and the chance for relapse is great.) Beltzer remains clean a year later, with one short relapse. His life has improved, his mind has cleared, and he hopes to return to local politics. But he wonders if people will have faith in him as an elected official after his addiction.

While Beltzer snorted his prescription opioids, twenty-eight-year-old Tiffany Turner injected hers. Turner lives in Scott County, Indiana, a small poverty-stricken county with a poor health-care system. She began taking prescription painkillers for severe back pain from four broken vertebrae she suffered during an auto accident. She needed the drugs to function at work and soon became hooked.

At about this time, officials in Scott County identified not only a high rate of opioid addiction among its residents but also a sudden outbreak of human immunodeficiency virus (HIV, the virus that causes acquired immunodeficiency syndrome, or AIDS). Investigators from the CDC traced the outbreak of HIV to county residents who were dissolving Opana (oxymorphone) pills and injecting them. Opana is a powerful prescription painkiller available only by prescription. People steal it or sell their own prescriptions on the street. Some residents were injecting Opana up to twenty times a day, sharing needles with others. This is a sure way to pass diseases such as HIV and hepatitis, a serious liver disease.

In response, medical officials looked for ways to address the addiction crisis, inadvertently creating other problems. For example, the county's only pain treatment clinic, which prescribed opioids as part of its treatment plans, shut down. Many local doctors stopped prescribing opioids altogether. Turner could no longer get her prescription painkillers. She felt she had to self-medicate to keep her job and pay her dying husband's medical bills. "I went to the street [for drugs]," she said. There, she bought Opana for twenty-five to thirty dollars per pill and began injecting it.

Turner injected drugs for two years. She was lucky. She tested negative for HIV and managed to get off Opana. She volunteers at a needle exchange clinic and tells her story at substance abuse education events in Scott County. The nearly two hundred people who developed HIV were eligible for treatment under the state's Healthy Indiana Plan, which provides treatment, testing, and medications.

ADDICTION DOES NOT DISCRIMINATE

Addiction can affect anyone, regardless of age, race or ethnicity, gender identity, class, or geography. Data from the CDC shows, however, that during 2002 to 2015, white Americans were about twice as likely to die from a drug overdose (mostly from opioids or from taking prescription painkillers and heroin together) as were African Americans. The same data indicates that white Americans are four times more likely to die of a drug overdose than are Hispanics. "Even in more racially diverse areas, like Long Island [New York] and New Jersey, this epidemic is very white," said addiction expert Kolodny.

"Drug overdoses are driving up the [overall] death rate of young white adults in the United States to levels not seen since the end of the AIDS epidemic more than two decades ago," science journalist Gina Kolata and editor Sarah Cohen wrote in the *New York Times*. In contrast, overall "death rates for blacks and most Hispanic groups continued to fall."

Kolodny suspects that racial stereotyping impacts the disproportionally higher overdose deaths among whites. "What's happening is we're overexposing whites to prescription opioids [by overprescribing]. Doctors prescribe narcotics more cautiously to black patients. [This is because doctors] may be more worried about addiction or diversion of the pills onto the [illegal] market if the patient [is] black."

Kolodny's conclusions are not new. Studies have consistently found that doctors are far less likely to prescribe opioid painkillers to African American patients than to whites for back or abdominal pain, for example. A study published in 2011 found that some African American patients may underreport the severity of their pain for several reasons. They're more likely to attribute pain to personal inadequacies than are white people. Black people may fear doctors won't believe them. Additionally, African Americans are more afraid than whites of opioid addiction. The study concluded that physicians were a major contributor to the racial disparities in the way pain is treated. This

"I used my privilege to 'pass.' My life as a stay-at-home mom was the perfect disguise. There are millions of us addicts disguised as regular people. We're not all rock stars: We're your neighbor or your sister. We're in the pickup line, waiting for our kids. We're on the PTA. . . . My name is Jen. I'm a stay-at-home mom. And I'm an addict."

—Jen Simon, Washington Post, *2016*

is related to their limited awareness of their own cultural beliefs and to common stereotypes regarding pain and its treatment in minority groups.

Overdose and addiction crises are not new to the United States. Yet the opioid crisis of the twenty-first century has gained an unusual level of media attention. According to some critics, this is because the problem is hitting mainstream white America hard. For example, the editorial staff of the *New York Times* pointed out that "Congress has historically treated drug abuse as a [disease] afflicting mostly poor, minority communities, best dealt with by locking people up for long periods of time. The epidemic of drug overdose deaths currently ravaging white populations in cities and towns across the country has altered this line of thinking, and forced lawmakers to acknowledge that addiction is a problem that knows no racial barriers and can be best addressed with treatment."

When the crack cocaine crisis hit the United States in the mid-1980s, it impacted mostly black Americans in low-income inner cities. Communities responded through law enforcement, targeting dealers and users as criminals. Get-tough programs around the country made it easier for law enforcement and courts to sentence Americans to long prison terms for even the most minor drug offense. By the twenty-first century, many experts in the US health-care community, within government, and in the legal establishment agree that it's time to move drug abuse out of the criminal justice system and into the public health-care system, where addicts can be treated and rehabilitated rather than punished.

AMERICAN INDIANS

Although white Americans are hit hardest by the opioid and addiction crisis, American Indians are at increased risk for addiction. Sarah Gaskill is a child protection social worker who has worked with American Indian families in Minneapolis, Minnesota. That area has a large concentration of urban American Indians. "The US government waged cultural genocide against American Indians until the 1970s," Gaskill says. "The government took children from their families and tribes and placed them in boarding schools and foster families. Officials stripped the children of their cultural identity, forbidding them from speaking their indigenous languages, from wearing traditional clothing, and from practicing their religions. Some did not experience healthy parenting skills to pass on to their own children."

American Indians were also forced onto reservations, and with limited resources and opportunities, many families fell into deep poverty and have never recovered. A report from the US Bureau of the Census published in 2013 found that the poverty rate for American Indians was 27 percent compared to the poverty rate of 14 percent for all Americans and 12 percent for whites only. "In the twenty-first century, American Indians still experience social and economic discrimination," Gaskill says. "Historical trauma such as this contributes to depression and puts American Indians at higher risk for addictive behaviors." More than 18 percent of American Indians and Alaska Natives aged twelve or older use illegal drugs—higher than any other group in the United States. A study of eighth- and tenth-grade American Indians showed they used two to three times more OxyContin and heroin than other teens. And in Minnesota, nearly five times more American Indians die of opioid overdoses than do other groups.

James Cross was born to parents affiliated with the Anishinabe and Dakota tribes. Because of their parents' alcoholism, he and his brother, Gerald, were taken from their family and were adopted and raised by a white family in Minneapolis. James and Gerald Cross spent much of their adult lives in gangs and in prison for drug-related activities. They robbed drug dealers in Minneapolis and nearby Saint Paul to sell the drugs on reservations in northern Minnesota. The brothers would use meth, opioids, and weed along with their customers. Now clean for more than ten years, James Cross works to win back the trust of elders and community leaders. "It's hard to be Native American in the community and show people you changed because you ruined the community . . . so many times with your actions of criminality or drugs." Overdoses are common in the community where he works. In one weekend, he learned of ten nonfatal opioid overdoses at Little Earth in Minneapolis, the only American-Indian-

James Cross (*center*) and his brother, Gerald, hold a poster for the Natives Against Heroin group at the Little Earth housing project in Minneapolis. The group holds traditional talking circles to invite addicts to open up about their experiences. The group offers help finding treatment and has broader goals to intervene in gang retaliation and other violence.

focused housing project in the country. Experts say additional research is needed to better understand how best to identify and treat addiction among American Indians.

BOTH GENDERS AND ALL AGES AT RISK

Research shows that women and men use and respond to drugs differently. Men are more likely than women to use almost all illicit drugs and to have higher rates of use and dependence. For example, 13 percent of men and 7.3 percent of women reported illegal drug use in a large 2014 study. Women begin abusing drugs at lower doses than do men, but drug use more quickly escalates to addiction among women. Women increase their dose of heroin, in particular, more rapidly, and they become addicted in a shorter period of time than do men. However, women tend to seek treatment sooner than men do. Women may be more susceptible to cravings and relapse, two major aspects of recovery. The reasons for these differences are not clear. Studies in animals suggest that both genetic and hormonal factors, as well as emotional and psychological differences between the genders may be responsible.

Drug abuse, addiction, and overdose deaths cut across all age groups. In a 2015 feature article about the US heroin epidemic, Sports Illustrated reported that 11 percent of high school athletes had used prescription painkillers for recreational purposes by the time they graduated. However, older Americans are not immune to drug abuse, addiction, and overdose. Many people sixty-five and older take prescription opioids such as OxyContin, Percocet, and fentanyl for chronic conditions including lower back pain and arthritis. Hospitalizations for misusing opioids have increased fivefold among middle-aged and older Americans. In fact, the CDC says that Americans between forty-five and fifty-four have the highest death rates from opioid overdoses. "Some [older people] have very severe, intractable pain," Kolodny said "They are able to find doctors to prescribe them all the opioids they might want."

Are these middle-aged and older people addicted to their painkillers? Kolodny says, "They're feeling agonizing pain [and] if they take the opioid, the pain goes away. They believe the opioid is relieving their underlying pain problem. What's probably happening is that the opioid is treating their withdrawal pain." He says that when people take several doses of opioids each day, physical dependence can begin in as few as five days. Both dependence and tolerance grow stronger over time, and a person's ability to function begins to decline.

Nearly one-fifth of people aged sixty-five and older who take opioids for chronic pain may abuse them or become addicted to them, according to one study presented by the American Academy of Addiction Psychiatry. Dr. Joseph Garbely is the medical director of a Pennsylvania drug treatment center with a drug rehab unit for seniors. He says, "Caretakers oftentimes miss the signs and symptoms of a substance-use disorder [among seniors]. Doctors do too, and often aren't asking the questions when seniors are there for their monthly checkups." Friends, family members, as well as health-care professionals can be on the lookout for abuse and misuse of opioids in older adults. The signs include receiving medications from multiple doctors, requesting early refills, reporting their pain medications have been lost or stolen, and appearing unkempt or impaired.

DYING FOR A FIX

When Prince, widely hailed as one of the most innovative musical superstars of all time, died on April 21, 2016 he was just one of sixty-two people who died that day from an opioid overdose. Friends reported that Prince Rogers Nelson had taken opioids for years because of hip pain related to his athletic stage performances. The medical examiner who investigated Prince's death found that he died of an accidental overdose of fentanyl.

A story in the *Washington Post* in August 2016 said that the pills were found in a bottle labeled with the ingredients in Vicodin. Prince

Prince is one of thousands of Americans who have died of opioid overdose. For example, Steve Rummler died in 2011 of an accidental opioid overdose after struggling with addiction brought on by efforts to manage his chronic pain. His mother, Judy Rummler is the cofounder of the Steve Rummler Hope Foundation, an organization that works with chronic pain patients. Prince died under similar circumstances in 2016. Many experts point out that Prince, like Rummler, suffered from a disease—addiction to prescription painkillers.

probably didn't know what he was taking. During his stellar career, Prince won an academy award, seven Grammys, and a Golden Globe Award. Sometimes it takes the death of a Prince to make people sit up and take notice.

"Prince's death will help to remove the stigma attached to overdose primarily because his death received so much attention from the media," said Judy Rummler, founder of the Steve Rummler Hope Foundation, an organization that works with chronic pain patients.

Drugs that Americans commonly abuse fall into two broad categories:

1. *Depressants* include prescription painkillers (opioids), prescription tranquillizers (benzodiazepines), and heroin. These drugs relax people by slowing the heart and breathing, sometimes to the point of death.
2. *Stimulants* include cocaine and methamphetamine. They excite users by speeding up the heart and breathing, sometimes to the point of death.

According to the CDC, more than fifty-two thousand Americans died of drug overdoses in 2015, including prescription painkillers, heroin, benzodiazepines, cocaine, as well as other legal and illegal drugs.

What does an overdose look like? Depressants and stimulants cause very different symptoms.

Depressant overdose: People who overdose on an opioid medication may experience nausea and vomiting. They show confusion and slurred speech. The pupils of the eye constrict to pinpoint size. Muscles relax, including chest muscles that help with breathing. The heart rate slows down, and breathing becomes shallow and slow. Fingernails and lips can turn blue due to a shortage of oxygen. The person may become unconscious—difficult or impossible to awaken. Breathing can stop completely, and if that happens, the heart soon stops as well.

When first responders reach an overdose victim, they can administer

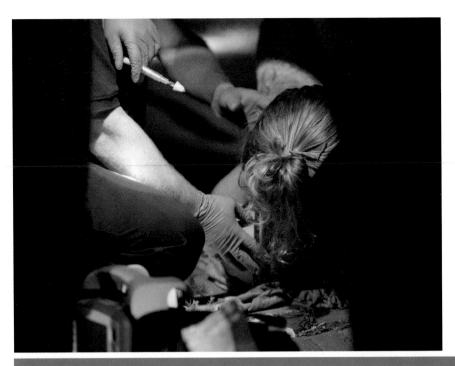

Paramedics administer a dose of the opioid antidote Narcan (naloxone) to a twenty-nine-year-old woman after she overdosed on heroin. When she regained consciousness, she told the responders that she knew the heroin she was taking that day was especially strong.

naloxone. This is the specific antidote (a medication that counteracts the effects of another medication) for an opioid overdose. They can inject the drug or spray it into the nose. The drug forces the body's opioid receptors to let go of the drug to help the brain "remember" how to breathe again. Naloxone works equally well for heroin or prescription painkiller overdoses. The lifesaving medication can reverse the effects of an opioid overdose within two to five minutes, although additional medical care is also required. Without cardiopulmonary resuscitation (CPR) and medical intervention, the person is likely to die. Naloxone is so effective and so safe that a prescription is not required to purchase it at many pharmacies across the United States.

FIVE THINGS TO KNOW ABOUT OPIOID OVERDOSES

1. You don't have to be addicted to be at risk for an opioid overdose. An opioid overdose can happen to anyone at any time. Risk factors for opioid overdose include taking high doses of the drug and taking it with alcohol or other drugs such as tranquilizers or sleeping pills.

2. An overdose is less likely when people take opioids *exactly* as prescribed by their doctors. People are at high risk of overdose if they stop taking opioids and then suddenly resume them or if their doctors change their prescriptions to something stronger.

3. Be alert to the warning signs of an overdose. Watch for shallow breathing, slow heartbeat, or bluish tint to the lips or nails. Call 911 immediately—even if you're not sure.

4. Giving the right medication can save the life of a person who overdoses on opioids. Naloxone (brand name Narcan) almost immediately reverses an opioid overdose. Emergency responders and many police officers are trained to use the drug.

5. Take action before a tragic overdose occurs. Intervene if someone you know or love is at risk for addiction or overdose. Suggest they go to Narcotics Anonymous (NA) meetings. Encourage them to see a doctor or therapist for help. Encourage them to enroll in an inpatient rehab program. If you can't persuade them on your own or are afraid to speak out, ask for the help of another trusted friend, adult, or family member to make the case with you. Don't give up. Your friend or family member's life is at stake.

Stimulant overdose: Cocaine and meth overdoses cause thousands of deaths in the United States each year. According to the 2014 National Survey on Drug Use and Health, about 1.5 million Americans used cocaine that year, and about 569,000 people used meth. While the US government doesn't track overdose deaths for every drug, it does collect that information for cocaine. About 5,500 Americans died of cocaine overdose in 2014. Experts think that the number of people who die of meth overdose is lower than that from fatal overdoses of heroin, prescription opioids, or cocaine. An estimated 500 people died of meth overdoses in 1998, the last year that the US government tracked meth overdoses. Both meth and cocaine increase dopamine levels in the brain (as do heroin and prescription opioids).

Because meth and cocaine are stimulants, symptoms of overdose are similar. They include the following:

- rapid heart rate
- chest pain
- delusions and paranoia
- headache
- agitation
- a dangerous increase in body temperature

People who overdose on meth or cocaine will have large, dilated pupils. They can die from seizures, heart attacks, and strokes due to high blood pressure. No antidote is available to reverse stimulant overdoses. In the emergency room (ER), doctors give sedatives to overdose patients to calm them and to decrease heart rate and blood pressure. Ice blankets and medications may also help decrease body temperature. Long-term use of stimulants can result in kidney failure, which may be fatal as well.

Generally, hospital personnel who treat overdose patients will recommend admission to a drug treatment program when patients are stable. Many health-care organizations and private treatment centers offer toll-free numbers for addicts who are seeking assistance in recovery. The National Alcoholism and Substance Abuse Information Center has a 24-7 toll-free line at (800) 784-6776. The center offers confidential online contact as well. The US government's Substance Abuse and Mental Health Services Administration (SAMHSA) receives about twenty-eight thousand calls a month for help at its referral line at (800) 662-4357.

NEW MEDS, NEW DANGERS

Even though deaths from prescription opioid overdoses continue to rise, pharmaceutical companies continue to develop new opioids. For example, in 2006 the US Food and Drug Administration (FDA) approved Opana, a painkiller twice as strong as the older drug OxyContin and ten times more potent than morphine. The pharmaceutical company that developed Opana claims the drug provides an alternative to patients who develop a tolerance for other painkillers. The company also says that the twelve-hour dosing schedule for Opana is more convenient than medications that require more frequent dosing.

In 2013 the FDA approved an extended-release opioid painkiller called Zohydro (hydrocodone), which is 25 percent more powerful than Opana and five to ten times stronger than Vicodin. Experts around the nation spoke out against the release of Zohydro, saying in a letter to the FDA, "In the midst of a severe drug addiction epidemic fueled by overprescribing of opioids, the very last thing the country needs is a new, dangerous, high-dose opioid." Kolodny was among those who did not support the new drug, saying, "It's a whopping dose of hydrocodone packed in an easy-to-crush capsule. It will kill people as soon as it's released."

In 2014 the FDA approved Hysingla, an extended release form of hydrocodone that is twice as powerful as Opana. It has physical and chemical properties that make it more difficult to prepare for snorting or injecting. Unlike some other opioids, patients only need to take Hysingla once a day.

ABUSE DETERRENT FORMULAS

Several pharmacy companies have developed new formulas to make it more difficult for an abuser to prepare tablets for snorting or injection. These formulas are known as abuse deterrent formulas. One example is the time-release formula. Capsules made this way contain dozens of tiny pellets that release the medication over a period of hours. This decreases the risk of an abuser using the medication for a quick high.

The *New England Journal of Medicine* found that these changes do reduce the abuse of that specific drug. Yet users turn to other opiates that are made without the abuse deterrent formulas. Generic versions of any drug are cheaper than brand name drugs, so many people choose them instead. However, generic opioids do not yet have abuse deterrent formulas. And insurance companies do not usually cover brand name abuse deterrent preparations, which can cost far more than generics.

Drug manufacturers say new opioids promise better results with less risk to users than older medications. Yet the increasing number of opioid overdose deaths suggests otherwise. Alex Lawson is the executive director of Social Security Works, an organization with a goal of safeguarding the economic security of people on Social Security. In the *Huffington Post*, he wrote about the financial goals pharmaceutical companies work toward. "Pharmaceutical companies put profits before public health and the result is billions [of dollars] for them and broken lives, drug addiction and death for the American people."

After intense criticism from experts and the American public, the FDA issued a statement in 2016 saying that the FDA is deeply concerned about the epidemic of prescription opioids. It also released an action plan designed to reduce the impact of opioid abuse in the United States.

According to Dr. Robert M. Califf, the FDA's top official, the new policy does the following:

- It increases transparency in the approval process for opioids and provides for public input.
- It improves communication with the medical community.
- It requires drugmakers to provide better information on the risk of abuse associated with long-term opioid use.

Califf called the policy, "a framework for how FDA can better do its part to confront the opioid epidemic."

BY THE NUMBERS

» About sixty-two Americans die from prescription painkillers and other legal and illegal opioids each day.

» White Americans are about twice as likely to die from a drug overdose as African Americans and are four times as likely to die of a drug overdose as Hispanics.

» About 11 percent of high school athletes have misused prescription painkillers by the time they graduate.

CHAPTER FOUR
FROM PRESCRIPTION DRUGS TO HEROIN

Alisha Choquette had everything going for her during her first year of high school in Stonington, Connecticut. She was a cheerleader, dated the quarterback of the high school football team, partied on the weekends with her friends, and still kept up her grades. Then a close family friend died. "I was extremely anxious about having to attend the wake. One of my friends handed me two pills and said they'd help me get through it. This was the day I met and fell in love with the love of my life—opioids."

Choquette says, "I remember the feeling I got from taking these pills. They made me feel as if nothing else in the entire world mattered and all I wanted to focus on was chasing that initial warm rush. All the anxiety associated with life's trials and tribulations was gone. It was as if I'd morphed into an entirely new person. It was a feeling I wanted to have for the rest of my life—a feeling I would

> "AMERICANS, CONSTITUTING ONLY 4.6% OF THE WORLD'S POPULATION, HAVE BEEN CONSUMING 80% OF THE GLOBAL OPIOID SUPPLY AND . . . TWO-THIRDS OF THE WORLD'S ILLEGAL DRUGS."
>
> —Drs. L. Manchikanti and A. Singh, *Pain Physician*, 2008

go to any lengths to chase."

It wasn't long before Alisha was stealing painkillers from the medicine cabinets of any house she entered, including those of family and friends. "By the end of my sophomore year, getting high became more of a priority for me than going to school. I left school every day right after checking into homeroom." Things got worse after she graduated. She used her mother's debit card to steal thousands of dollars from her mother's checking account. A family member was in a bad auto accident, and Choquette stole her painkillers. "I needed to feed my own habit. I wasn't concerned with what she would do when she needed her painkillers and they were gone."

After fighting addiction to prescription painkillers and heroin for several years, Alisha Choquette turned her life around. Twenty-nine years old and drug-free, she's a licensed chemical dependency professional working as a substance abuse counselor at a men's residential drug treatment facility.

Choquette got pregnant when she was twenty years old. "I kept telling myself I was going to stop taking drugs, but the addiction was just too powerful. I would lay awake at night rubbing my belly and promising the baby that I would do better. The next morning, I'd wake up with every intention of not taking drugs, but the craving would take over and I'd give in to temptation. I loved my unborn child more than anything in this entire world, except for my true love, opioid pain pills. I had promised myself that once my baby came into this world, I was going to change my life around, but instead my addiction just grew stronger."

After the baby was born, child protective services soon placed Choquette's daughter with relatives because she was not capable of caring for the child. She stole a doctor's prescription pad and tried writing prescriptions for opioids for herself. She was arrested, tried, and sentenced to prison. Her sentencing judge offered her a diversion program instead—a chance to clear her name if she went through treatment and remained clean for one year. She agreed, but someone in the treatment program gave her heroin. She became addicted to heroin and was kicked out of the program. "Heroin was less expensive than the pain pills, and you can get much higher for a cheaper price. I overdosed numerous times on heroin. After multiple admissions into treatment facilities and several incarcerations, I was finally able to stay clean long enough to complete the court program and clear my criminal record."

Things looked as if they were turning around for her. She started college and saw her daughter on the weekends. Yet when her father died, addiction took over her life again. Anxiety overwhelmed her, and a doctor prescribed the tranquilizer Xanax to calm her. "I filled the prescription and in less than twenty-four hours the one-month supply of Xanax was gone. I was once again chasing a feeling that took over my life." Choquette had four DUIs in one month while on Xanax and was sentenced to prison for a year. Meanwhile, her mother died. Choquette spent most of her prison reflecting deeply on her life. When she was released, she had the determination to turn things around permanently.

"Being a drug addict is a lifelong commitment that I would not wish on anybody," she says. "Addiction does not discriminate. It doesn't care where you come from, what you look like, who you know, or what kind of person you are. Anyone can become addicted and once they are, they become someone they never would have believed they were capable of becoming."

FROM THE MEDICINE CABINET TO THE STREET

Like so many opioid addicts, Choquette stole the prescription drugs she wanted from the medicine cabinets of friends and family before turning to heroin. And like her, nearly nine out of ten people who began using heroin since 2006 were white, and many were middle-class or upper-class

Americans. "Most of the heroin users now, their first opioid exposures are the prescription drugs," said Dr. Wilson Compton, deputy director of the NIDA. "That's true for at least 80 percent of today's heroin addicts. That's very different than 30 or 40 years ago, when the first opioid was heroin."

How do people move from swallowing pills to injecting heroin? Many begin with legitimate prescriptions for opioid painkillers obtained from reputable doctors after an injury. That's what happened to Roman Montano. A gifted baseball player in Albuquerque, New Mexico, Montano needed minor surgery to repair a broken bone in his foot when he was a junior in high school. His surgeon gave him a prescription for OxyContin, and Montano quickly healed from his painful injury. But a few months later, he and his friends used a stolen credit card to make a purchase at a mall and were caught. Even though it was Montano's first offense, the baseball coach kicked him off the team.

Many people who are addicted to prescription painkillers doctor shop, looking for more than one doctor to write out a prescription for narcotics. Or they may steal prescriptions and fill them at multiple pharmacies. Responsible health-care providers, insurance companies, and pharmacies are building better prescription drug monitoring programs to avoid this type of misuse. As prescriptions for narcotics become harder to get, many addicts are turning to injecting heroin instead.

Angry and depressed, Montano remembered how great OxyContin had made him feel. Soon he was deep into prescription painkillers, using them along with marijuana and alcohol at parties. In his senior year, Montano switched from OxyContin to heroin, which gave him the same high at a lower price. He smoked it. He injected it. He died at twenty-two from a heroin overdose in his car, with the motor still running and a syringe hanging out of his arm.

Addicted to painkillers, patients may return time and again to their doctors to renew their prescription. At first, doctors may do so. But when physicians refuse to write further prescriptions, some people begin doctor shopping. They visit other doctors to complain of pain in the hopes of obtaining more prescription painkillers. If a doctor doesn't know a patient is seeing other doctors, that doctor may write a prescription. In fact, the addict may receive prescriptions from multiple doctors at the same time, getting hundreds of pills each month. To prevent this, states and counties are working to better coordinate prescription records with doctors and pharmacies.

Addicts have other tricks too. They may show up repeatedly at hospital ERs with complaints of severe pain. Hoping that busy staff won't ask too many questions, they may be able to obtain a prescription for pain medications there. If that fails, addicts may turn to the street to buy prescription painkillers from dealers. However, drug dealers charge thirty dollars or more for a single opioid tablet. It doesn't take long for an opioid addict to discover that heroin—at five dollars for a small bag in some cities—is cheaper than a tablet and delivers a high much more quickly.

HEROIN EPIDEMIC

More Americans than ever are using heroin. The United Nations released a report in June 2016. The report documented that one million Americans were using heroin as of 2014 and that heroin deaths have more than quadrupled since 2010. Many experts agree that heroin use is increasing as it becomes more difficult for people to obtain prescription painkillers. "Heroin use has been increasing markedly by all measures," Compton said.

"Abuse rates are going up. Death rates are going up. . . . It qualifies as an epidemic by anyone's definition."

According to the CDC, nearly everyone who uses heroin also uses at least one other drug. Most people use three or more. For example, people addicted to alcohol are twice as likely to be addicted to heroin as are nonalcoholics. Cocaine addicts are fifteen times more likely to be addicted to heroin than are people who don't use cocaine. And people addicted to opioid painkillers are forty times more likely to be addicted to heroin than people who don't take opioid painkillers. The number of overdose deaths from prescription painkillers and other legal and illegal opioids in the United States rose from sixteen thousand to nearly twenty-two thousand between 2010 and 2015. Heroin deaths skyrocketed from three thousand to nearly thirteen thousand in that same period.

What explains the sharp rise in heroin use and deaths? The demand for heroin has increased as Americans have more difficulty getting prescription painkillers legally and affordably. Instead, they turn to heroin. With the increase in demand for heroin, drug trafficking has risen dramatically. And with heroin flowing into the country (primarily from Mexico) in large amounts, the price of the drug drops, making it even more desirable among addicts. "The trafficking and abuse of illicit drugs pose a monumental danger to our citizens and a significant challenge for our law enforcement agencies and health care systems," said Chuck Rosenberg, acting administrator for the US Drug Enforcement Administration. The DEA ranks prescription painkillers and heroin as the most significant drug threats to the United States.

A TALE OF TWO CITIES

Heroin affects many people in many parts of the country, both high-income and average-income cities. Darien, Connecticut, and Auburn, California, are two such contrasting cities. In the 2010 census, Darien had a population of 20,732, while Auburn was a bit smaller at 13,330. The average yearly household income in Darien is nearly $200,000. In contrast, Auburn's average annual household income is just over $54,000. What do these two very different cities, one on the East Coast and one on the West Coast, have in common? The heroin addiction and overdose crisis is going strong in both.

Mark lives in Darien. Michael lives in Auburn. Both young men are heroin addicts. Mark is in his twenties. He started snorting heroin as a teen, telling himself that he would never inject it. As Mark's addiction grew, he snorted ten bags of heroin a day. (The size of a bag of heroin varies. An average dose of heroin is 0.0035 ounces, or 0.1 grams.) Cost didn't matter to Mark because he came from a well-off family. When Mark needed more heroin, he just popped down to the Bronx (a borough of New York City) and picked up some from his dealer.

One day, Mark injected heroin. After that, "sniffing didn't cut it anymore. I [injected] wherever, every day. [Addiction] happens in the blink of an eye," Mark said. He overdosed twice, and both times awoke to firefighters working to revive him. Mark was lucky. The first responders gave him naloxone to reverse the effects. "If it wasn't for that, I wouldn't be here talking to you right now," he told a reporter.

About fifteen of Mark's friends died from heroin overdoses. Heroin is in the streets. It's in Darien High School. "A lot of parents think, no, not my baby," Mark said. Mark didn't receive any referrals to rehab after his two overdoses, but he managed to find treatment. Under a doctor's supervision, he's on a prescription medication that works to fight heroin cravings, and it has helped. "I feel better than I was. Waking up sick every day is not a life. Eventually people get sick and tired of being sick and tired."

Meanwhile, in Auburn, Michael had been a promising basketball player since elementary school. In high school, he played basketball for his school's team. By tenth grade, he was using Norco (a combination of acetaminophen and hydrocodone) to treat the aches and pains that go along with being an athlete. "They made me feel comfortable, and they came from a doctor," he said, "so I figured they were all right." By the eleventh

OPIOID WITHDRAWAL

Prolonged use of opioid drugs changes the brain's chemistry. Suddenly stopping the drug causes extremely painful symptoms known as withdrawal. In fact, the agony of withdrawal is what keeps many addicts from getting clean. While each person is different, many people will experience these symptoms:

1. Within the first twenty-four hours of stopping the drug, people experience muscle aches, restlessness, anxiety, runny nose and eyes, excessive sweating, inability to sleep, and yawning.
2. Symptoms worsen during the second day without the drug. They include severe abdominal cramping, diarrhea, goose bumps, nausea and vomiting, dilated pupils, blurry vision, rapid heartbeat, and high blood pressure.
3. Symptoms begin to improve within three days and are usually gone within a week.
4. The intense craving for the drug lasts much, much longer.

grade, drugs were everywhere. "Kids you would never expect to do drugs were taking pills," Michael said. Parents unknowingly supplied most of the pills by not locking up their own prescriptions.

Michael moved on from Norco to crushing and smoking OxyContin tablets. But he discovered that heroin costs a lot less and gave him a better high. He smoked heroin the first time before a basketball game. "I played great. No anxieties, no pain. I loved it," he said. Soon Michael used heroin before every game. "I couldn't play without it. I needed it. I was hooked." It was easy to get heroin in Auburn. "If you can come up with $40 a day, you can maintain [your habit] and your parents will never know."

DEATH IN THE EMERGENCY ROOM

The emergency room door whooshed open as a middle-aged man rushed in with his teen son Josh in his arms. He screamed for help and yelled that his son wasn't breathing. The dad said that Josh was sixteen and that he suspected a friend had given his son heroin. Nurses placed Josh on a gurney and quickly wheeled him into an exam room.

Dr. Tom Zimmerman is a physician who worked in the ER of a small community hospital in the Sierra Nevada foothills of Northern California for fourteen years. He witnessed scenes like this far too often. (Josh is a composite of several patients that Zimmerman treated in the ER.) A nurse put electrodes on Josh's chest and connected him to a heart monitor. Another nurse held an oxygen mask over Josh's face to get him breathing again. "His heartbeat and blood pressure were very low and his pupils were constricted," Zimmerman said. "Because Josh wasn't breathing, his skin was blue. These findings could certainly indicate a heroin overdose."

Within minutes, Josh had intravenous (IV) lines in both arms to keep him hydrated and to allow the ER staff to give him emergency medications easily. "We gave him the opioid reversal agent Narcan twice without any improvement in his condition. We pumped IV fluids into his veins and inserted an endotracheal tube [a tube through the mouth and into the lungs] to provide better ventilation and more oxygen.

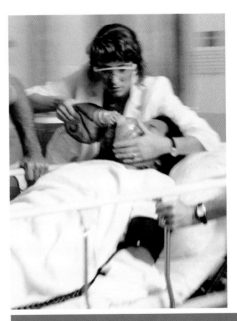

When dealing with a patient with an apparent opioid overdose, emergency room staff work fast to administer Narcan, fluids, and oxygen.

A SHORT HISTORY OF HEROIN

For thousands of years, people across the globe have made products from the opium poppy (*below*) to reduce pain and to feel a sense of well-being.

- As early as 3400 BCE, Sumerians grew and used opium in Mesopotamia (modern-day Iraq and Kuwait).

- Greek physician Hippocrates (460 to 370 BCE) believed opium was helpful for "women's diseases," which, at the time, referred to just about anything to do with women's health, such as menstruation, infertility, and vaginal infections.

- British doctor Thomas Sydenham introduced laudanum, a mixture of opium, wine, and herbs, in 1680. People—especially women—used it for a wide variety of ailments including pain, anxiety, and insomnia.

- German scientist Friedrich Sertuerner refined morphine from opium in 1803. In 1827 the German drug company E. Merck began manufacturing morphine for widespread use.

Over the next half hour, nurses put other tubes into Josh, one through his penis and into his bladder to obtain a urine sample to identify what drugs he'd taken. Another tube went into his stomach to empty it and to prevent vomiting and the possibility of inhaling stomach contents into the lungs. Josh received an electrocardiogram (ECG) to evaluate his heart. He also had multiple blood tests, a chest X-ray to evaluate his lungs, and a CT [computerized tomography] scan of his head to rule out bleeding into the brain."

Josh started having seizures, Zimmerman said. "We gave him

- Scottish doctor Alexander Wood learned to inject morphine in 1843.
- By the mid-nineteenth century, growers in the United States were raising opium poppies for morphine. American doctors widely prescribed morphine and opium for patients. Drugstores and grocery stores sold it, and Americans could even purchase opium by mail. US drug companies made more than six hundred patent medicines containing opium or morphine. Some were sold to reduce teething pain in infants. American doctors called opium God's Own Medicine and used it for patients suffering from pain, sleeplessness, heart disease, and diabetes. Doctors also used it to "cure" insanity.
- In 1874 British researcher C. R. Wright discovered how to turn morphine into heroin.
- In the late nineteenth century, American doctors recommended giving alcoholic patients heroin rather than alcohol because they said it improved their lives.
- By 1903 heroin addiction had risen to alarming rates in the United States. Congress banned the importation and use of opium in 1905. In 1923 the US Treasury Department's Narcotic Division banned all illegal drug sales.
- Most of the heroin used in the United States comes from Mexico.

anti-seizure medications. The seizures stopped, but Josh remained unresponsive. By then, his pupils were dilated, a sure sign of significant cerebral anoxia [lack of oxygen to the brain]. We put him on a mechanical ventilator to regulate the oxygen being pumped into his body." When test results came back, the chest X-ray and CT scan were normal. But the ECG showed heart damage. Blood tests revealed that Josh's liver and kidneys were failing. The urine test was positive for opioids.

"It . . . became obvious what had happened," Zimmerman said. "The patient had overdosed on heroin, stopped breathing, and gone into shock.

It must have been some time before Josh's dad found him, long enough that lack of oxygen caused irreversible damage to his brain. The low blood pressure reduced blood flow to his liver and kidneys, causing them to fail. The Narcan was too late to help."

Josh's mother and sisters arrived at the ER and gathered with Josh's father around the gurney. "They were beside themselves with grief," Zimmerman said. The ER staff transferred Josh to the intensive care unit. After a few days, specialists determined Josh had irreversible brain damage, total organ failure, and no hope of recovery. "We stopped his oxygen and medications and he passed away," Zimmerman said. "Josh was another victim of a society obsessed with getting high, and a young person not understanding the danger of narcotics."

BORN IN WITHDRAWAL

"I was in labor, in the bathroom, shooting heroin, about to give birth to my child," Clorissa Jones, a young heroin addict in recovery, told a reporter. "A lot of people were like 'how could you dare do that to your child?' But nothing mattered except for getting high."

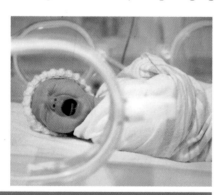

Babies born in withdrawal experience the same excruciating symptoms an adult would go through when withdrawing from an opioid. Among many symptoms, the babies are extremely agitated and irritable, unable to sleep, and express their intense discomfort through a shrill cry.

Jones gave birth to Jacoby, her first baby. Because his mother was an addict, Jacoby had heroin in his system too and went into withdrawal a few hours after his birth. This story happens every day in the United States. According to the NIDA, a baby is born suffering from opioid withdrawal every twenty-five minutes in the United States—five times more babies than in 2000. The US Department of Health and Human Services reports that about twenty-seven

RISE IN DRUG-DEPENDENT NEWBORNS

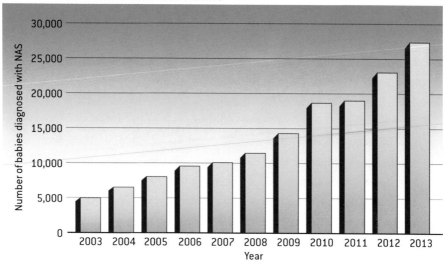

Source: Reuters analysis of US Department of Health and Human Services data

This chart, based on data from the US Department of Health and Human Services, shows the significant and fairly rapid rise in the number of US newborns born with neonatal abstinence syndrome, or NAS.

thousand such births occur per year, and the number is on the rise.

But these are not addicted babies because addiction implies a set of specific behaviors. "We want to avoid the stigma of calling these newborns addicted," says Earl R. Washburn, MD, a California pediatrician with experience caring for infants born to opioid-addicted mothers. "More importantly, the mother's addiction is not the infant's issue. The newborn's problems are related to withdrawal." Doctors use the term *neonatal abstinence syndrome* (NAS) to describe what Jacoby and babies like him go through—withdrawal from whatever drug the mother was using while she was pregnant.

A baby with NAS may look normal at first, Washburn says. "The timing of symptoms related to withdrawal depends on what the mother was taking, how much, and how long prior to delivery she last used. The start of the infant's withdrawal ranges from hours to a couple of days after birth. Once withdrawal starts, the baby has tremors and twitches, clenched muscles, and irritability. The baby's cry is not like that of a typical newborn: it's high-pitched and shrill." Newborns with NAS have difficulty feeding. They may have a fever and sweat profusely, and they often experience frequent diarrhea and vomiting. Normal newborns sleep most of the day. Babies with NAS cannot sleep because of their agitation and the unpleasant symptoms they experience. Instead, they're awake most of the time.

Not every hospital can properly treat babies with NAS, so staff must transfer these babies to hospitals with specialized neonatal intensive care units. These units have the equipment and trained staff to manage the unique needs of these babies. These infants stay much longer in the hospital than healthy newborns. "All newborns are monitored closely," Washburn says, "but those known to be exposed to maternal opioid use are monitored and assessed even more frequently. Nursing staff minimizes stimulation by handling the infant less often, keeping lights low, and noise at a minimum. Doctors usually give the baby tiny amounts of morphine [which is chemically related to heroin] by mouth every few hours to manage the withdrawal. Babies with NAS may also receive benzodiazepines, medications that help to relax muscles and control seizures, if present."

Experts used to believe that a baby born with NAS would suffer lifelong consequences such as brain damage, developmental delays, and learning disabilities. However, research hasn't demonstrated a link between these conditions and babies born to addicted mothers. "We don't think that they have any neurodevelopmental delays just from going through withdrawal," Dr. Leslie Kerzner, medical director of the Special Care Nursery at Boston's Massachusetts General Hospital, says. She has tracked some of these children for years. "In most kids, the brain is very plastic [flexible], and they kind of rewire."

Washburn says it's important to understand the difficulties addicted mothers and NAS babies face. "Addicted mothers are not evil. They don't want their babies to go through withdrawal. Like all mothers, they want healthy babies." But opioid addiction is typically so powerful that for pregnant women such as Clorissa Jones and Alisha Choquette, it overpowers their ability to make wise decisions for the health of their unborn babies.

Ideally, every addicted mother should be referred to drug treatment programs after delivery and assessed to determine if she is capable of caring for the child. Some hospitals do a good job of this, following provisions of the federal Keeping Children and Families Safe Act of 2003. That act requires states to set up systems to ensure that a medical staff alert child protection workers about newborns who are suffering from withdrawal symptoms at birth. Yet a 2015 Reuters news agency investigation found that most states either ignore that provision or lack the funding to take necessary action. In other cases, laws are contradictory or confusing. For example, some states don't require hospitals to report drug-dependent newborns if the mother was taking methadone, painkillers, or other narcotics prescribed by a doctor.

BY THE NUMBERS

» People addicted to opioid painkillers are forty times more likely to be addicted to heroin than those who are not addicted to opioid painkillers.

» Eight out of ten new heroin addicts started with prescription painkillers.

» In the United States, a baby who is suffering from opioid withdrawl is born every twenty-five minutes.

CHAPTER FIVE
PATIENTS AND DOCTORS IN THE MIDDLE

It took the jurors two weeks to reach their verdict: guilty of second-degree murder. But the defendant wasn't a drive-by shooter nor was she driving under the influence. Instead, Hsiu-Ying "Lisa" Tseng, a forty-six-year-old doctor practicing medicine in Los Angeles, California, became the first American physician to be convicted of murder for recklessly overprescribing drugs. Three young men died when they overdosed on the opioid pain medications she had prescribed for them. In previous years, medical examiners and law enforcement officials had notified Tseng that more than a dozen of her patients had overdosed and died. Yet according to the prosecutor, Tseng did not change her prescribing habits. Her husband, also a doctor, said she viewed these calls as FYI (for your information) notices that required no action on her part.

During the eight-week trial in September 2015, Tseng's attorney said she was a well-meaning

"PAIN AFFECTS MORE AMERICANS THAN DIABETES, HEART DISEASE, AND CANCER COMBINED. AN ESTIMATED ONE HUNDRED MILLION AMERICANS LIVE WITH CHRONIC PAIN."

—American Academy of Pain Medicine, 2016

Los-Angeles-based general physician Dr. Hsiu-Ying "Lisa" Tseng (*right*) is serving a sentence of thirty years to life for the second-degree murder of three of her patients who overdosed. The sentencing judge stated that Tseng had blamed patients, pharmacists, and other doctors instead of taking responsibility for her reckless overprescription of drugs. Some doctors support the sentence, while others fear it will lead physicians to be too cautious about prescribing painkillers.

physician who had gotten in over her head while dealing with manipulative, drug-seeking patients. Los Angeles County Superior Court judge George G. Lomeli disagreed, saying that Tseng ran a reckless assembly-line type of practice while patients and their families suffered. The prosecutor told jurors that Tseng gave patients—including an undercover drug agent posing as a patient—prescriptions for powerful narcotics even after patients told her about their addiction. Seventy-seven witnesses testified at the trial, and the prosecution presented 250 pieces of evidence.

At her sentencing hearing in February 2016, Tseng apologized to victims' relatives who were in the courtroom. "I'm really terribly sorry. I have been and forever will be praying for you. May God bless all of you and grant comfort to all who have been affected by my actions." Lomeli then sentenced Tseng to a prison sentence of thirty years to life for her crimes.

DOCTORS IN THE SPOTLIGHT

Tseng is not the first physician turned drug dealer, and she likely won't be the last. For example, on May 18, 2016, a grand jury indicted Dr. Narendra K. Nagareddy, an Atlanta-area psychiatrist on three counts of murder and fifty-nine counts of unauthorized distribution of painkiller prescriptions. Nagareddy had been arrested in January and was free on bail. Authorities rearrested him the day of the indictment and ordered him held without bail until his trial. Past autopsies confirmed that twelve of Nagareddy's patients had died of prescription drug overdoses. An unnamed former patient said, "You just tell him [Nagareddy] what you want and you get it."

And in 2015, the US Justice Department announced the biggest ever drug-related takedown in the DEA's history. Agents arrested 280 people, including doctors and pharmacists, for scheming to distribute huge quantities of addictive painkillers in four southern states.

The CDC says physicians are one major cause of prescription painkiller overdoses. "Prescription drug overdose is epidemic in the United States," CDC director Frieden said in an official report in 2014. "All too often and in far too many communities, the treatment is becoming the problem." By one estimate, doctors write so many prescriptions for painkillers that every adult in the United States can have a bottle of them.

> "Prescription drug overdose is epidemic in the United States," CDC director Frieden said in an official report in 2014. "All too often and in far too many communities, the treatment is becoming the problem."
>
> —Tom Frieden, CDC director

Researchers from the American College of Physicians looked at nearly three thousand adult patients who suffered nonfatal opioid overdoses while taking long-term opioid medications for chronic pain. Even after an overdose, nine out of ten of the patients continued to receive prescriptions for opioid painkillers from their doctors. And 17 percent of those patients overdosed again over the next two years. Authors of the study said the findings show the challenges doctors face trying to balance the risks and benefits of prescription opioids for patients with chronic pain. The authors said better tools are needed to identify and treat patients at risk for opioid use disorders.

Medical and law enforcement experts say only a tiny fraction of doctors knowingly prescribe unnecessary opiates. Cases such as Tseng's and Nagareddy's may make doctors reluctant to prescribe pain medications to those who need them. Dr. Peter Staats, a physician who specializes in caring for patients with severe pain, said, "When you use the word 'murder,' [in relation to a prescription-drug overdose] of course it's going to have a chilling effect [on doctors]."

The negative media attention to the overprescription of addictive narcotics concerns many physicians. In the past, opioid medications were generally used only for severe pain, such as may occur with cancer or following major surgery. Many other forms of chronic pain were ignored. Washburn says, "It wasn't that long ago that there was significant and appropriate criticism of medicine for failing to treat people's pain adequately." Medical personnel worried about patients becoming addicted to opiate medications. Physicians prescribed them cautiously, and even in hospitals, nurses administered narcotics reluctantly for fear of addicting their patients.

Starting in the 1990s, public opinion and medical culture shifted so that more people received these powerful medications for chronic pain. Doctors began to prescribe opioids for medical conditions such as low back pain, severe arthritis, or damaged nerves. Drug companies often pressured doctors to prescribe the powerful products, to be proactive with addressing pain, and to treat it aggressively. The use of opioids grew tenfold in twenty years. With the current addiction and overdose crisis in the United States, doctors face ever-increasing pressure to cut back on prescribing opioids for chronic, long-term pain.

"Now there's an outcry that physicians are overusing opioids," says Washburn. "That makes it harder for legitimate doctors to write prescriptions for patients who could benefit from them. Doctors may be in a real bind if they start prescribing anything other than low levels of opioids. Everybody feels uneasy about this." Are doctors overmedicating patients in chronic pain? Undermedicating them? "These things are a two-edged sword. They cut for good and for bad. I don't think anybody has an answer yet that really works very well, but I do know that you can't have it both ways," Washburn says.

PATIENTS SPEAK OUT

Of the estimated one hundred million Americans living with chronic pain, one-quarter of them say it severely limits their quality of life. Many of these people are concerned about the spotlight on opioid use. Lauren Kramer is a forty-five-year-old woman with several degenerated discs in her lower spine. In the past, she experienced severe low back pain on a daily basis and could barely walk. Surgery could not repair her discs and over-the-counter medications offered little help.

Kramer went to a doctor specializing in the treatment of chronic pain. "When my doctor first looked at the MRI [magnetic resonance imaging] scan of my spine he said, 'I cannot even imagine the amount of pain you're in.' Since surgery couldn't help, all he could offer was to help control my pain with medications," she says. She's taken opioid medications daily for four years. "I'm very thankful that the small doses I take allow me to function relatively normally. I'm also grateful that I don't seem to be developing a tolerance for the medications; I'm taking the same dose that I started with."

Only a few close family members and friends know that Kramer takes narcotic painkillers. "These people know I'm not an irresponsible addict, and they don't judge me for taking these drugs. There are many people who aren't drug abusers who take long-term opioid drugs for legitimate medical conditions," she says. Kramer values her privacy and is also aware of the

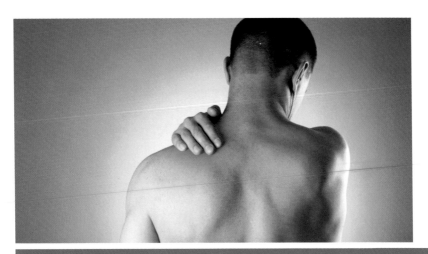

Many Americans initially seek prescription drugs for relief from pain associated with a severe injury, arthritis, nerve damage, or other painful physical conditions. For many of these people, the drugs allow them to live their daily lives relatively free from suffering. Others discover that they have become dangerously addicted to the drugs. Researchers are looking for pain-relief medications that do not carry the risk of addiction.

stigma of taking such medications. "It isn't fair to assume that all opioid users are addicts who are trying to get high. I don't want to be high or to impair my thinking. I just want to be able to work, to drive where I need to go, and to function well enough that I can do some of the family things that most people take for granted," she says. "These drugs allow me to function without being in constant agony. I couldn't do these things if my back pain wasn't controlled."

Dr. Robert Kingwell is a retired physician and also a patient who takes opioids. One of the chemotherapy medications he received during cancer treatment years ago left him with generalized neuropathy—pain and numbness in the nerves of many parts of the body, especially in his feet. Also, a surgical procedure accidentally damaged his sciatic nerve—the long nerve that stretches from the lower spine down the back of each leg. "I used to require higher doses of pain medication during the first years after my cancer treatment, but my pain is less now than it was then.

NEEDED NO MORE

Unused or expired medications of any kind, especially prescription narcotics, are easily misused, stolen, or sold. Children may get into so-called childproof bottles and ingest liquids or pills that can critically injure or even kill them. Confused or elderly people may take the medication by mistake.

Because of these dangers, experts urge Americans to dispose properly of expired or unused drugs—and to keep all medications away from children by locking drugs up or storing them in a secure location. Each community has different ways to dispose of prescription drugs. For example, some pharmacies accept them. Walgreen's and Rite Aid plan to install disposal stations (*shown below*) in hundreds of their stores so that customers can safely discard unneeded and expired medications. Many counties have programs to collect and dispose of painkillers at drop-off sites. Law enforcement agencies sponsor take-back days. Some pharmacies may also offer mail-back envelopes to assist consumers in safely disposing of their unused medicines through the US mail. The DEA holds a National Prescription Drug Take Back Day each April 30.

The FDA recognizes that easy, community-based disposal of unneeded medications is not available to everyone. If this applies to you, check the FDA website for more information about how to safely dispose of unused medications. According to the FDA, the best way to dispose of medications if they must go into the household trash is to do the following:

1. **Crush pills and mix them with an absorbent, unpleasant substance such as dirt, kitty litter, or used coffee grounds.**
2. **Place the mixture in a sealed plastic bag.**
3. **Throw the bag into the household trash.**

Drugs flushed down the toilet may end up in drinking water. Sewage treatment plants cannot filter out medications. Even so, the FDA recommends that if a person has no way to dispose of a drug safely, they should—as a last resort—flush the opioid medications down the toilet. The risk to drinking water, according to the FDA, is far lower than the risk of even one person overdosing on someone else's easy-to-reach pills.

I take four to five doses of hydrocodone each day, about 25 milligrams in total. A lot of people take much more," he says.

Kingwell's pain begins in the afternoon and worsens as the day goes on. "The pain can be a particular problem at night because it hurts the most when I go to bed. My prescription reduces the pain enough so that I sleep better but does not eliminate it. That's enough to allow me to enjoy my life and to function more normally," he says. "If I go too long between doses, my pain increases. However, I don't crave the medication, nor do I feel any euphoria at these low doses. I have no evidence of tolerance. Even so, I'd be delighted if I didn't require these medications anymore."

Kingwell does not prescribe opioid medications for himself. (Some doctors may abuse the system and prescribe for themselves.) "I never expected different rules for me because I was a physician," he says. "I respect the power that opioids have for both good and bad. It's a balance between taking enough to manage the pain, but not using too much. We must treat opioids with care and respect. They can help people, but they can also ruin lives. The same can be said of automobiles, which cause thousands of deaths every year. We don't outlaw cars, but we do regulate their use."

MONITORING THE MEDS

Even as opioid deaths continue to rise across the country, doctors are beginning to prescribe them less often in many states. "The culture is changing," said Dr. Bruce Psaty, a researcher at the University of Washington in Seattle who studies drug safety. "We are on the downside of a curve with opioid prescribing now." The government is tightening rules on some opioid medications, pharmacies are coordinating medication records in some states, and medical schools are teaching medical students the benefits and dangers of opioid use.

Some physicians say some patients may be undertreated for pain in the future, while others may continue to receive too many opioids. For example, doctors in some states prescribe painkillers more frequently than in other states. A 2014 CDC report found that doctors in Tennessee wrote nearly twenty-two times more prescriptions for oxymorphone than doctors in Minnesota. Do patients in Tennessee have more pain than those in Minnesota? The CDC says the factors driving the increase in painkillers in certain states include these:

- "Health care providers don't always agree on when to use prescription painkillers and how much to prescribe." For example, painkillers are prescribed more often in southern states than in other parts of the country.
- "Some of the increased demand for prescription painkillers is from people who use them non-medically . . . sell them, or get them from several doctors at the same time."
- "Many states report problems with for-profit, high-volume pain clinics (so-called "pill mills") that prescribe large quantities of painkillers to people who don't need them medically." In these states, prescriptions for opioids are far higher than in states with fewer pain clinics. It may be difficult to regulate these clinics or to close them down because, in some cases, the clinics are legitimate medical practices.

In 2015 a CDC panel wrote that "primary care providers report concern about opioid pain medication misuse, find managing patients with chronic pain stressful, express concerns about patient addiction, and report insufficient training in prescribing opioids." In response to the need for more training, the CDC published its first-ever guidelines for prescribing opioid medication for chronic pain in March 2016. The document is aimed specifically at the nation's primary care physicians. These physicians prescribe nearly half of all opioid medications (specialists prescribe the other half), yet often have little training in how to use them for chronic pain.

"We know of no other medication routinely used for a nonfatal condition that kills patients so frequently," said Frieden. "We hope to see fewer deaths

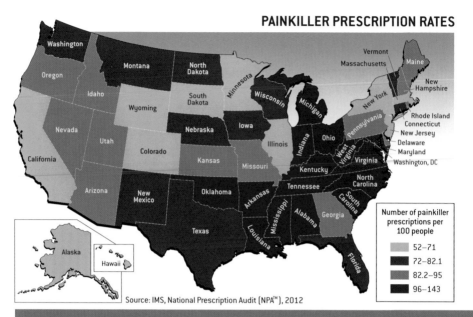

PAINKILLER PRESCRIPTION RATES

Number of painkiller prescriptions per 100 people

- 52–71
- 72–82.1
- 82.2–95
- 96–143

Source: IMS, National Prescription Audit (NPA™), 2012

This map, based on CDC data, shows the varying painkiller prescription rates state by state. Some states prescribe at far higher rates than others.

from opiates. That's the bottom line. These are really dangerous medications that carry the risk of addiction and death."

Kolodny believes the guidelines are a game changer that doctors are likely to follow. "For the first time, the federal government is communicating clearly that the widespread practice of treating common pain conditions with long-term opioids is inappropriate," he said. "The CDC is making it perfectly clear that medical practice needs to change because we're harming pain patients and fueling a public health crisis."

The guidelines clarify that opioids are seldom needed for more than a week when used for acute pain such as after an injury or surgery. Chronic pain, on the other hand, is defined as noncancer pain that lasts longer than three months. This type of pain is most often due to musculoskeletal pain such as arthritis and to back and neck problems. One study showed that more than 11 percent of American adults report having daily pain and that

3 to 4 percent of them take long-term prescription opioid medications for their chronic pain.

The guidelines, which are voluntary recommendations for physicians, cover three broad areas:

1. *When to begin or continue opioids for chronic pain.* Doctors should first try methods of managing chronic pain such as counseling, physical and occupational therapies, and non-opioid medications such as acetaminophen and anti-inflammatories such as ibuprofen. A doctor and patient should together establish realistic treatment goals with the understanding that if started, opioids will be discontinued if benefits do not outweigh risks and there is not a significant decrease in pain and an increase in function.

2. *Selecting opioid dosage, duration, and discontinuation.* Doctors should start by prescribing the lowest possible dose, gradually increasing the dose only if necessary. "When opiates are used, start low and go slow," the CDC's Frieden said. The doctor should evaluate the patient within four weeks of starting opioid medications and should determine every three months whether ongoing therapy is necessary.

3. *Managing risk and harm.* Doctors should ask about patients' previous use of opioid medications as well as past substance abuse problems or overdoses. Doctors should consider routine urine or blood testing to be sure that the patient is taking the opioid as prescribed and that the person is not also using other medications or drugs that have not been prescribed. Sometimes such tests show that the patient is not taking the prescribed opioid at all, which can mean that the person is selling the drug or giving it to others.

Not all experts agree with the guidelines, however. Chris Hansen, president of the American Cancer Society's Cancer Action Network, feels the guidelines don't consider the importance of pain management for cancer survivors such as Kingwell, who continue to experience severe pain years after successfully completing cancer treatment. "Pain does not end when an individual completes treatment," Hansen said. "Most often, cancer patients deal with lasting effects from their disease or treatment including pain for a significant period of time or indefinitely." Patients have different pain tolerances. Doctors currently have no objective tool for measuring pain and must rely on patients' descriptions of their own pain level. This can make it even more difficult for physicians to know when to prescribe opioid painkillers and when not to.

Kramer feels she is doing everything right in managing her pain. "I go to a pain clinic once a month and the doctor carefully monitors my condition and my opioid use," she says. "I signed an opioid use agreement in which I promised not to abuse or sell the pills, plus the doctor's office does random urine tests to monitor my usage. I take this agreement very seriously and understand that if I violate any of its terms I can go to jail as well as being banned from the pain clinic."

Yet Kramer finds some of the regulations troublesome. "It's more difficult for me because the US government, which has no business telling doctors what they can or cannot prescribe for their patients, has implemented new rules that require doctors to encourage patients to take non-opioid medications and to question patients more frequently about their compliance with the opioid contract," she says. "It's wrong for the government to assume that everyone who takes opioids for legitimate reasons is an irresponsible addict who abuses these drugs. Doctors are very aware that some people who try to get prescriptions for these drugs are abusers who just want to get high. The good doctors can spot these fakers a mile away, and they not only refuse to accept them as patients, but in some cases, they also notify police if they suspect a patient of selling prescription drugs."

Kingwell, who has used opioid medications for many years, says, "Before the change in the prescribing rules, refills could be handled over the phone.

THE OPIOID PRESCRIPTION CONTRACT

Most doctors who prescribe opioid painkillers for chronic pain will require their patients to sign a contract before receiving a prescription. Contracts may vary from doctor to doctor, but in general, patients must agree to do the following:

- Keep all appointments with their doctor and not ask for additional medication between appointments.

- Keep the medication in a safe place and away from children, knowing that if it is lost or stolen, the doctor will not write another prescription until the next month. If the medications are stolen, a patient is generally required to file a police report.

- Refrain from selling or sharing the medication.

- Fill all prescriptions at the same pharmacy.

- Refrain from seeking prescriptions from other doctors.

- Refrain from using any illegal drugs such as heroin.

- Recognize that breaking any provision of the contract may result in termination of care and opioid medication.

The newer rules require that I visit my doctor's office for a written refill every month. This is a minor annoyance, but the extra step is something that I accept as part of taking care of myself." Kingwell's physician does not require him to sign an opioid use agreement. "I've demonstrated a very consistent pattern of medication use for quite a long time, but if I had to sign such an agreement, it would not be a problem for me."

Kingwell adds, "I think that a physician must carefully supervise any sort of chronic medical treatment. I'm always checking myself for any signs of addiction problems, but I rely on my personal physician to monitor me. She carefully watches how frequently I get refills and sees me at regularly scheduled office visits. I think this sort of medical surveillance is very important. In a way, it comforts me to know there is someone who is counting the days and the pills and watching me."

BY THE NUMBERS

» Nine out of ten patients who overdosed on prescription opioid drugs continue to receive prescriptions for them from their doctors.

» Doctors write so many prescriptions for narcotic painkillers that every adult in the United States could have a bottle of them.

» About 11 percent of Americans report having daily pain.

CHAPTER SIX
PRESCRIPTION FOR A BETTER FUTURE

"**N**o one plans to be a drug addict," says forty-five-year-old Leeann Nielson. "You don't wake up one morning and decide to become addicted to drugs. Addiction happens so gradually that you don't realize how much you need your drug of choice until you try to stop using. Once you're an addict, your addiction never takes a day off. It's always on your mind. Satisfying your craving becomes your full time occupation."

Nielson graduated from college at the age of twenty-three with a professional degree in the health-care field. While in college, she had used alcohol and marijuana but never hard drugs. That changed at a graduation party, where she met a law student and started living with him. "We occasionally did cocaine," she said, "but our relationship was unhealthy and he was sometimes abusive. I began drinking more and

"A MISCONCEPTION IS THAT ADDICTIONS ARE ALMOST IMPOSSIBLE TO OVERCOME. IF YOU FAIL ONE REHAB WITH ONE VERSION OF TREATMENT, IT DOESN'T MEAN YOU CAN'T GET BETTER, IT MEANS YOU HAVE TO TRY AGAIN."

—Dr. Adi Jaffe, psychologist and addiction specialist, 2010

Talk therapy is a key component in drug rehabilitation programs. Working toward and maintaining sobriety requires support from professionals, friends, and family. Most recovering addicts will also benefit from attending support groups such as Narcotics Anonymous after rehab.

smoking pot daily." They married, and the abuse grew worse. As the violence escalated, so did her drinking. She and her husband had two small children. The violence worsened, and she left the marriage. "I had to leave without my children because my husband threatened to hurt me or even to kill me if I tried to take them."

Nielson turned to methamphetamine to cope with her painful divorce and the loss of her children. "When I was high on meth I felt energized and didn't think about my children. I didn't need food or sleep. But when I wasn't using, my depression was deep. I felt dizzy, nauseated, irritable, exhausted, and shaky." Her new boyfriend showed her how to inject meth. When she became pregnant with her third child, Nielson briefly stopped using meth but resumed her habit soon after the baby was born. However, she lost her job after surgery for a work-related injury and could no longer afford the drug. "During my addiction, I never resorted to theft to support my habit."

By then Nielson had married the father of her new baby, and the couple decided to stop using. "We had an opportunity to join a faith-based recovery program run by two Protestant pastors and their wives." Nielson and her husband joined the program voluntarily. Courts—whose judges sentence addicts to jail or to treatment programs—recognized the program as a drug treatment center and sent numerous residents there directly from court or from jail. "The program consisted of about seventy families who were housed in a rented motel. Being accepted into the program was the beginning of our new lives," she says.

Through this program, she and her husband found sobriety. The faith-based component was part of what helped them on their journey to recovery. She says, "My husband and I have been clean and sober for fifteen years. We continue to rely on our faith and the support we found in the program. It's frightening to have an addiction to something you know is dangerous, illegal, and ruining your life. I felt trapped in the cycle of addiction when I was using and although recovery wasn't easy, it was so much easier than dealing with my addiction every day. I feel very thankful to have escaped that lifestyle."

> "I felt trapped in the cycle of addiction when I was using and although recovery wasn't easy, it was so much easier than dealing with my addiction every day."
>
> —Leeann Nielson, recovering drug addict

CULTURE MATTERS

Nielson asks, "Why did my husband and I escape the addiction cycle while so many others try and fail multiple times to get clean? One reason is because I feared the risky addictive lifestyle; another is because I was able to return to work while so many others struggle to re-establish their work history. However, the primary reason is my faith, which gave me and my husband the strength to leave the darkness of addiction behind."

A faith-based program was right for Nielson and her husband, and she believes it's the reason she and her husband achieved and maintain their sobriety. In addition, women—especially those with young children—and family groups such as hers—have a better chance of success in recovery programs that take family needs into account. For example, she and her husband had different needs than a younger single person in a substance abuse rehabilitation program might require. For Nielson, those needs included a supportive, family-style environment with flexible treatment sessions and day care options.

People of different ethnicities have unique needs as do older people. For example, inpatient rehab programs for seniors remove them from their homes and isolate them from their peers. A rehab program may not be able to address chronic health conditions such as diabetes and heart disease that some seniors live with. Seniors may do better with day treatment programs. There, they spend several hours every day in a treatment facility but return to their own homes at night.

"People are more likely to have success in their recovery if their needs are addressed through culturally specific models," says social worker Sarah Gaskill. James Cross agrees. As an American Indian and recovering addict, he strongly believes recognizing an individual's culture helps recovery. " [Because of the] historical trauma we've been through, I think we need to have our own programs specific for Natives," he said. "Use our culture, use our flute music, use our . . . pow wow music, round dance music, use our own theories from our forefathers and our elders."

The SAMHSA refers to cultural competence as "the ability [of counselors and other providers] to honor and respect the beliefs, languages, interpersonal styles, and behaviors of individuals and families receiving services, as well as staff members who are providing such services." Being aware of—and responsive to—individuals' cultures improves commitment to services, strengthens relationships between individuals and health-care providers, and improves outcomes.

REHABILITATION CAN WORK

At least two million Americans enter a drug rehab program each year. Recovery is hard. Very hard. Jaffe, a psychologist, lecturer at the University of California–Los Angeles, author, and a recovering addict says that addicts can be treated, but not easily and definitely not quickly. "Treating addicts with 30-day programs is a horrendous idea. Almost nobody changes a habit in 30 days. The NIDA has long recommended a minimum of 90 days inpatient residential treatment. Most people don't get that, and rehab for a month is just not enough," he says. "The longer the addiction and the more entrenched, the longer you need to be away from it."

People may voluntarily enter a rehabilitation program for their addiction. Sometimes a drug court will order admission to rehab instead of incarceration. The United States has more than three thousand drug courts. These are courts where addicts face trial and sentencing after being arrested for drug-related charges. Depending on the severity of the crime, these courts will sometimes sentence an addict to treatment and regular drug-test monitoring as part of a probation plan.

If a judge sentences an offender to prison, treatment can continue there. Once released, treatment continues while the offender is on parole. Teams consisting of judges, social workers, addiction professionals, attorneys, and law enforcement officers help manage the court-ordered and prison programs. The programs are targeted to the needs of adults, youths, and families and are very successful. For example, the National Institute of Justice, the research and evaluation agency of the US Department of Justice, reports that participants in drug court-ordered programs have lower rates of rearrest and less criminal activity than offenders who did not attend a drug court program. Participants also report 56 percent to 76 percent less drug use and are less likely to fail drug tests. Drug courts save the legal system as much as $6,200 for each participant because fewer people reoffend if they take advantage of court-ordered treatment programs.

Regardless of how people begin rehab, the NIDA points out that no single treatment is appropriate for all individuals. Programs must address the multiple needs of the person, not just the drug use. For example, the most successful programs provide a combination of therapy and services to meet needs defined by age, race, culture, gender, pregnancy, sexual orientation, housing, and employment. Matching individuals to the right programs is crucial to their ultimate success in kicking their habits and returning to a full life.

Some, but not all rehab programs, take place in an inpatient setting. Some are entirely outside of a facility. Some use medications, while others don't. Most rehab programs start with detoxification (detox—clearing drugs out of the body). It would be difficult if not impossible for a person who is high to participate in and benefit from a rehab program. Stopping drugs suddenly may be potentially dangerous for some people and is best managed by a physician, often with medications to ease withdrawal symptoms. Detox can occur in either an inpatient or outpatient setting depending on the patient's condition.

By itself, detox does little to change long-term drug use. It is only the first step in rehab. After detox, patients have these options (unless a court orders otherwise):

- **Long-term residential treatment.** People live in a nonhospital facility that provides twenty-four-hour care. The frequent sessions with professional counselors and interaction with other addicts go a long way toward recovery. Many people will choose one of the fourteen thousand residential treatment centers in the United States. Wealthy individuals (think addicted movie stars) can select accommodations as luxurious as a five-star hotel. Other programs, such as the one that Nielson and her husband entered, took place in a rental hotel run by religious-oriented counselors. Regardless of the facility, the NIDA says that less than ninety days in residential treatment (or any program) is of limited effectiveness.

- **Short-term residential treatment.** These intensive residential programs may last three to six weeks. The brief stay must be followed by extensive outpatient therapy and participation in a self-help group such as Narcotics Anonymous (NA).
- **Day treatment programs.** People spend several hours a day at a rehab center. For some patients, these programs can be as effective as residential programs.
- **Outpatient treatment programs.** These programs allow people with family or job obligations to continue their normal lives to the extent possible while getting the treatment they need to overcome their addictions.

Talk therapy combined with medication greatly increases the chance of recovery from addiction.

1. **Individual therapy** can help people learn new communication and life skills to attain and maintain sobriety. This type of therapy can also encourage people to pursue or continue their education and to return to a job they may have lost because of their addiction.
2. **Group counseling**—meeting with others in addiction recovery— reduces the feeling of isolation by providing peer support and improving social and problem-solving skills.
3. **Family behavior therapy** allows family members to participate in a person's recovery, to express their concerns, and to share their hopes. A positive family support system improves the chance for recovery.
4. **Cognitive therapy** helps addicts recognize, avoid, and cope with triggers that lead to their drug use.

Many people know about Alcoholics Anonymous (AA). Founded in 1935, AA is the oldest twelve-step recovery program in the world. Programs like AA encourage each participant, within a group environment that protects

Group therapy allows people in treatment to share stories and get support from others who are experiencing similar struggles.

a person's privacy, to acknowledge and complete twelve specific steps as they move toward an alcohol-free life. NA is a program for recovering drug addicts based on AA strategies. "The twelve-step model has its limits," says social worker Gaskill, "but it is successful in helping recovering people establish a sober community, which is key to long-term sobriety. Also the twelve-step model is a program that practices forgiveness and helps recovering people find a way to make amends."

AA and NA include a spiritual orientation, referring to a higher power as part of the journey to recovery. Some recovering people who self-identify as agnostic or atheist, or who practice a non-Christian religion prefer programs that don't mention a god. Instead, they use the power of other recovering addicts for inspiration and guidance.

How effective are drug treatment programs? According to the NIDA, the goal of treatment is to return a person to a normal, high-functioning life. While drug treatment programs may not "cure" some addicts, they can be as successful as treatment for diabetes, asthma, and high blood pressure—illnesses that are managed rather than cured. Overall, however, drug treatment programs reduce drug use and crime by 40 to 60 percent. They also reduce unemployment by 40 percent. They're cost-effective to the individual and to society. For example, every dollar invested in drug treatment saves approximately twelve dollars in health-care and crime-related costs. That's a win-win for the individual and for society.

MEDICATION-ASSISTED TREATMENT

Whether to treat opioid-addicted patients with medications to help them through withdrawal is a controversial topic among experts. Withdrawal medications—which work in slightly different ways—can ease cravings, depression, and anxiety. Yet patients can sometimes become addicted to the withdrawal medications or abuse them. So while many rehab programs offer medication-assisted treatment (MAT), others insist patients go cold turkey to get clean. However, research consistently shows that MAT, along with behavioral therapy, is the most effective way to recover from addiction and to prevent relapse.

These are the medications that doctors with rehabilitation programs use for patients in recovery. Patients see their doctors frequently and are monitored through urine tests.

- **Methadone** comes in a liquid or pill that patients must take in an approved outpatient methadone clinic each day. Its effects last about twenty-two hours. Methadone prevents withdrawal symptoms and reduces cravings by activating opioid receptors in the brain, causing some people to experience a mild high. The health-care staff supervises patients taking methadone. However, people may lie and say they need a higher dose, or they may continue to take heroin or opioid painkillers while on methadone. Both of these activities can lead to fatal overdoses. Still, studies show that patients on methadone are more than four times likelier to stay in treatment than patients who take a placebo (a fake medication). Methadone has been used to treat addiction since the 1960s, and it has proven very effective. However, some patients have to travel an hour or more each day to receive their dose. This and the cost associated with maintaining clinics, limit the availability of methadone treatment.

- *Buprenorphine* (brand name Subutex) works by relieving cravings. It activates opioid receptors in the brain although to a lesser extent than methadone. It produces only a very mild euphoria. Experts consider buprenorphine the gold standard—the preferred method—for treatment of opioid withdrawal. Buprenorphine comes in a tablet that melts under the tongue and is taken once a day. In May 2016, the FDA approved Probuphine, a buprenorphine implant. A doctor injects the implant—consisting of four, 1-inch-long (2.5-centimeter) rods—under the skin of a patient's upper arm. The drug eases cravings and withdrawal symptoms for six months. The long-lasting approach helps prevent abuse or diversion (giving or selling the drug to others).

- *Suboxone* (buprenorphine combined with naloxone) also reduces cravings along with the risk of diversion or abuse. It comes in tablets and a film that melts under the tongue and is taken once every twenty-four hours. Dr. Jeffrey Allgaier is an addiction treatment specialist who founded and heads several addiction treatment centers in the United States. He says, "Suboxone is six times safer than methadone," because its ingredients make it impossible to overdose. If addicts take an opioid while on Suboxone, they go into immediate withdrawal.

The naloxone in Suboxone forces opioid receptors to let go of the drug within minutes. Buprenorphine by itself and with naloxone are both prescribed only by physicians trained in the treatment of addiction.

- **Naltrexone** (brand name Vivitrol) blocks the euphoric and sedative effects of opioids such as heroin. Vivitrol binds to and blocks opioid receptors to reduce opioid cravings. There is no potential for abuse or diversion with naltrexone. If a person relapses and uses their drug of choice, naltrexone prevents the feeling of getting high. A physician or health-care professional injects a patient with Vivitrol once a month as part of an ongoing drug rehab program.

Vivitrol is an increasingly important part of rehab for incarcerated individuals. At least fifty state prisons and dozens of jails offer the drug to inmates, most of whom detox cold turkey while imprisoned. In some prisons and jails, inmates receive monthly injections during their entire incarceration. In other cases, the drug is given once on discharge to ensure the recovering addict will not relapse for at least thirty days. For example, prison officials at Cape Cod's Barnstable County Correctional Facility in Massachusetts offer Vivitrol to each addict on discharge. The national rate of rearrest for drug offenders is 77 percent within five years of release. Those who receive Vivitrol when leaving Barnstable have had only a 9 percent rate of rearrest during the four years the program has been offered. About two-thirds of the nation's 2.3 million inmates are addicted to drugs (or alcohol), so beginning rehab while incarcerated can greatly improve chances of staying clean upon discharge for many people.

Among patients who receive MAT, the rate of death from all causes associated with addiction—including overdose, auto accidents (such as those caused by driving while high), and HIV/AIDS infection (from sharing dirty needles)—is half that of patients who do not receive MAT. Far more people stay clean with MAT than without. Some patients may taper off their

A teen resident of Echo Glen Children's Center, a juvenile rehabilitation facility in Snoqualmie, Washington, kisses and hugs the dog she has trained. The facility offers behavior therapy, anger replacement training, cultural programming, sex offense, and inpatient chemical dependency treatment for youth offenders.

withdrawal medications over time, but others may require them for life to maintain normal function.

Not all withdrawal medications work the same for every patient, however. For example, William Hayes, a longtime heroin addict in Washington, DC, said methadone felt like a shadow of a heroin high and made him crave the real thing even more. Taking Suboxone instead of methadone eliminated his intense craving for heroin. "It's working!" he said. "I ain't been in trouble. I ain't been in jail. I ain't using. Ain't doing none of that. I feel like a regular person."

Even though MAT has a proven track record of success, only 40 percent of the 2.5 million Americans who could benefit from MAT receive it. One reason is cost. Withdrawal drugs are expensive, and not all insurers pay for these drugs or may cover them for a limited period of time only.

A NEW NON-OPIOID PAINKILLER?

In 2012 a group of scientists at California's Scripps Research Institute announced they had discovered the atomic structure of the brain's opioid receptors. Knowing the atomic structure of the receptor is a bit like seeing a model of a building complete with windows and doors and closets and empty rooms. Opioids such as heroin and prescription painkillers must fit perfectly into every nook and cranny in every room of the building, or they won't work.

Based on this knowledge, an international team of researchers in California, North Carolina, and Germany announced in August 2016 that they had built a groundbreaking, non-opioid painkiller—on a computer! Knowing the atomic structure of the opioid receptor, scientists performed about four trillion virtual experiments simulating how millions of possible drugs could turn and twist in millions of different angles to fit into the receptors.

Researchers then used mice to test twenty-three drugs. Researchers wanted to see which would stimulate the opioid receptors to relieve pain without the side effects of opioids. The winner? A nifty little drug called PZM21. Dr. Brian Shoichet, a professor at the University of California–San Francisco, calls it "unprecedented, weird and cool." PZM21 tested in mice suggests it relieves pain and seems to lack the addictive qualities of existing opioids. Lab mice didn't crave the drug or tolerate electrical shocks to get more of it. They seemed to have little interest in it. It may be several years before PZM21 is tested in humans. But the potential for a nonaddictive, non-opioid drug for pain relief and MAT is substantial.

Some critics view MAT as substituting one addiction for another. Others believe that long-term use of withdrawal medication to manage addiction is as necessary as long-term use of blood pressure medication for heart patients or insulin for diabetes patients.

Another barrier to MAT is the limited number of trained physicians allowed to treat addicts with medication. *USA Today* points out that 877,000 physicians in the United States can legally write prescriptions for opioids as painkillers. Yet only 29,000 are authorized to prescribe medications to treat opioid addiction. Under the Drug Addiction Treatment Act of 2000, the US government allows doctors to treat thirty patients at a time with buprenorphine after eight hours of specialized training. Addicted patients have complex needs and require frequent monitoring, including periodic urine testing for drugs. However, after one year, a physician may apply to SAMHSA and obtain approval to treat up to one hundred patients at a time with MAT.

In July 2016, Congress passed a landmark bill allowing nurse practitioners and physician assistants to prescribe buprenorphine to patients. And in August 2016, physicians with specialized training in addiction medication or addiction psychiatry, who have prescribed buprenorphine to 100 patients for at least one year, can apply to increase their patient limits to 275. Patients will find it easier to participate in MAT programs with these new regulations.

OPPOSING MAT

People who oppose MAT ask, Why trade one drug for another? They point out that patients may sell or give away their prescribed withdrawal drugs or may take more or less of them than prescribed. An addict may stop the medications for a few days to get high on their drug of choice. Missing doses of a drug that controls withdrawal can quickly lead to a relapse in recovery. And some addicts cannot make the commitment to take a daily medication. "The narrow-minded approach for the past decade has been to simply expand access to methadone or buprenorphine and . . . call it treatment," US representative Tim Murphy of Pennsylvania says. "You can't call it treatment if we are simply swapping out a street drug for a synthetic, government-sanctioned one."

Some addiction experts are also against MAT. "When faced with a choice, who among us will not take the easiest route?" asked Dan Cain, who heads an agency that runs drug treatment programs in the Minneapolis area. "Taking a pill is certainly easier than self-examination and change. We are conditioned to look to pharmaceuticals to address issues (from obesity to high cholesterol) that are much more effectively addressed by lifestyle change." He also points out that while methadone and Suboxone may keep addicts from using opioid drugs, "they do nothing to inhibit use of benzodiazepines, methamphetamine, cocaine, marijuana, alcohol or any other mood-altering substance."

Opposition to MAT is dwindling because data shows that programs that do not include MAT are far less successful than those that do. Opioid addiction produces such intense cravings that sheer willpower alone is often not enough to stay clean. Cochrane is a trusted organization that gathers and summarizes data from many sources before making recommendations for physicians. One Cochrane analysis of eleven major studies found methadone to be significantly more effective than nonmedication approaches to recovery. A second Cochrane analysis of buprenorphine showed that it reduces illegal opioid use as well. "The abstinence-based model for opioid addiction is no longer considered an appropriate medical management," Dr. Jeffrey Allgaier said.

> "You can't call it treatment if we are simply swapping out a street drug for a synthetic, government-sanctioned one."
>
> —Tim Murphy, US representative, Pennsylvannia

HARM REDUCTION

The HIV/AIDS pandemic first surfaced in the 1980s. Activists, health-care workers, and policy makers argued that it would be far better to provide clean needles to drug users than to have the disease continue to spread. However, opponents feared that giving clean needles to drug addicts would only encourage more people to begin using drugs. Controversy swirled around needle exchange programs in the United States and other countries. More and more people came to believe that preventing the spread of HIV/AIDS benefited society as a whole. The needle exchange programs endured and broadened to include additional services.

The Harm Reduction Coalition has offices in California and New York. The group describes harm reduction as a spectrum of strategies ranging from safer and better managed drug use to abstinence and providing services such as medical care and housing to improve individual lives. Harm reduction theory accepts that illicit drug use is part of society. The program works to minimize harmful effects of drug use rather than ignore or condemn users. Harm reduction is a new way to think about addiction, a philosophy that recognizes that some addicts are not willing or may not be able to kick their habits.

Harm reduction realizes that addicts face a wide range of health risks, some of which can be minimized. For example, many addicts buy their drugs from street dealers, who often sell dangerously contaminated drugs. Many addicts have poor judgment, which leads them to practice unsafe sex and raises their chances of contracting HIV/AIDS and other sexually transmitted diseases (STDs). Addiction is also expensive, and when addicts run out of money, they may steal money or sell their bodies for sex, raising the risk of STDs, arrest, and prison time. Above all, addicts face the almost constant risk of deadly overdoses.

Harm reduction offers a controversial approach to help preserve the dignity of human life. What if heroin addicts could get their daily fixes from a nurse at a clinic instead of from a street dealer? What if they didn't have to rip off a convenience store to pay their dealers? That's what happens in Vancouver, British Columbia. The city's Providence Crosstown Clinic is the only facility in North America that offers heroin as prescription medication to addicts, along with a safe place to inject it. The government-funded program is known as heroin maintenance. It's for people who haven't been able to overcome their addiction with methadone or buprenorphine. "Many of our

Dr. Martin Schechter (*right*) was the head researcher for the Canadian-based North American Opiate Medication Initiative (NAOMI). This 2005 study came to the conclusion that heroin maintenance is an effective way to help chronic addicts safely manage their addiction. NAOMI led to the creation of a heroin maintenance facility in Vancouver, British Columbia. In this photo, Schechter is in the Vancouver clinic's injection room, which provides hard-to-treat heroin addicts with a clean, safe site for injecting under medical supervision. Because of the project's success, supporters want to expand it across Canada.

clients tell me it's the difference between life and death," says Dr. Scott MacDonald, lead physician at Crosstown.

"I'm . . . a better person," said Lynda LePretre, who spent more than twenty of her forty-eight years using heroin. While on the streets, she turned to sex work and drug dealing to pay for her habit. Now that she obtains medical-quality heroin from the clinic, she has time to work two part-time jobs. She's gained weight, and her general health has improved. "I'm more reliable now. . . . I'm not stressed all the time thinking about where my next hit is coming from."

The clinic also works for Dave Napio. "My whole life is straightening out," he told a reporter. Napio spent a total of twenty-two years in jail for drug-related crimes. "I'm becoming the guy next door." Instead of stealing jewelry to support his habit, Napio now spends his time making jewelry, working to turn his skill into a profession. He doesn't have to worry about getting HIV or hepatitis from dirty needles. Police no longer throw him into jail, and paramedics no longer rush him to the emergency room because he overdosed.

Some addicts are trapped in a seemingly endless cycle of jail time and overdosing. They are in and out of jail or prison for committing crimes to pay for their drugs. And many are in and out of ERs for repeat overdoses. Hospitals can often save people from death by overdose or refer people to rehab. Incarceration, however, is seldom a cure for addiction nor is it a threat that prevents people from using. Usually whether a drug is legal doesn't affect a person's decision to use it.

The City of Vancouver saw that the criminal justice approach wasn't working. "We tried to arrest our way out of [the rampant use of heroin] and that didn't work," Sergeant Randy Fincham of the Vancouver Police Department said. "Clogging up our courts and jails was not the solution." With the city's decision to set up a health-care model instead, fatal overdoses in the neighborhood where the clinic is based have decreased by 35 percent. Drug-related crime and infections have also dropped among clinic patrons. And the cost to treat addicts at the clinic is far less than the cost of emergency medical care and incarceration. Another positive aspect of the program is that addicts see the health-care staff daily. They are more likely to seek out other social service programs such as counseling.

"I'm . . . a better person. I'm more reliable now. . . . I'm not stressed all the time thinking about where my next hit is coming from."

—Lynda LePretre, recovering heroin addict who attends a heroin maintenace facility in Vancouver, British Columbia

The clinic's program has been so successful that supporters want to offer it in other Canadian cities. The Vancouver experience has profoundly changed the lives of the eight hundred addicts who inject at the clinic for the better. "We've seen people make dramatic changes in their lives," MacDonald said. "They don't have to hustle or do sex work anymore, and some are now able to go to school or to work." Without having to spend hours every day trying to score the next fix, addicts such as LePretre and Napio can use that time to improve their lives and contribute to their communities.

WILL HARM REDUCTION WORK IN THE UNITED STATES?

Opponents of harm reduction programs fear they enable addicts to keep using. It seems intuitively correct that making it easier and more convenient to support an addiction would only encourage continued use of the addictive drug. In the summer of 2016, a US congressional committee held a hearing titled, "America's Insatiable Demand for Drugs: Examining Alternative Approaches." MacDonald, the lead physician of the Vancouver heroin maintenance clinic, was one of four experts invited to speak.

When Senator Ron Johnson of Wisconsin asked MacDonald if his sites were magnets for drug dealers and crime, MacDonald answered, "There has been no increase in social instability around the clinics. There's been no 'honeypot effect,' where people come from other [areas] to seek the treatment." And when asked if the neighborhoods resisted the clinics, MacDonald said, "Having seen the success

> "More than $1 trillion down the drain—for nothing! . . . millions incarcerated . . . countless families and communities savaged. . . . Hundreds of thousands dead in drug wars from Asia to the Americas. Terrorists funded by drug money. Prisons packed. Gangs empowered. Governments intimidated and corrupted."
>
> —Ethan Nadelmann, executive director of the Drug Policy Alliance, in an editorial about the war on drugs in Rolling Stone, 2016

and the benefits both to the individuals and to the community [resistance has] fallen away now."

One of the invited speakers at the hearing was David W. Murray, formerly with the White House Office of National Drug Control Policy. He opposes a similar injection program in the United States. He says, "For the government to step into the role of officially providing addictive heroin to its citizens so transforms the relationship of the citizen to the government that we should fear it." The hearing was intended for governmental officials to listen to experts, so a new US drug policy was not established.

Some communities and organizations in the United States are implementing less controversial harm reduction strategies. Boston Health Care for the Homeless Program has a new program where trained staff supervises eight to ten addicts at a time after they've injected off-site. The staff monitors their condition and offers support and information about medical care and addiction treatment. The ultimate goal is to prevent overdoses among homeless addicts. Anyone needing medical care is taken to the hospital across the street for treatment.

The city council in Seattle, Washington, is considering a similar safe drug site. The mayor of Ithaca, New York, appointed a committee to consider building a site where addicts could safely and legally inject heroin. San Francisco is contemplating a comparable program. Harm reduction programs also can connect addicts to social services such as housing and medical care, offer education, and serve as a gateway to drug treatment services. The programs offer help in a nonjudgmental manner to aid in restoring the human dignity of the addict until that person is ready or able to get clean.

CHAPTER SEVEN
RELAPSE AND RECOVERY

Between 70 to 90 percent of recovering addicts experience at least one relapse, a temporary (or sometimes permanent) return to drug use. Some experience many relapses. Even so, more than twenty-three million Americans aged eighteen and older have overcome addiction to drugs or alcohol. Addiction expert Dr. David Sack says addiction is similar to other chronic diseases such as diabetes, asthma, and high blood pressure. Failure to follow medical treatment plans for those conditions also results in relapses that may be life threatening in some cases.

"Typically, addicts who return to drugs nearly always do so in response to drug-related cues, such as seeing drug paraphernalia or visiting places where they've scored drugs," Sack said. Addiction causes hyperstimulation of the brain's reward centers causing addicts to use again, to seek a repeat performance of the feel-good high they crave. "Repeated overstimulation of the reward centers causes long-term changes in how other areas of the brain function, including areas involved with memory, impulsivity, and decision-

> "ADDICTION RELAPSE IS COMMON. . . . NOT MANY PEOPLE SAY 'I WANT TO GET SOBER,' WALK INTO A TREATMENT CENTER, AND NEVER USE DRUGS AGAIN."
>
> —Dr. David Sack, addiction expert, 2012

making," he said. These factors help explain the often frequent relapses that so many addicts experience before they finally kick the habit. Relapse isn't a sign of failure, says Sack. It is to be expected, and it means that the addict must try again.

Most relapses occur within the first ninety days of recovery, which are the toughest for addicts. Because addiction physically rewires the brain, it takes weeks, even months, for the brain to repair itself and learn how to overcome the addiction. Anxiety and depression may have contributed to an addiction in the first place. These mental health stressors often worsen in the early days of sobriety. According to *Psychology Today*, an eight-year study of twelve hundred addicts and alcoholics found that the longer a person is clean, the greater the chance of continued sobriety. Study outcomes showed the following:

- Only about one-third of people remain sober during their first year of abstinence.
- However, after a full year of sobriety, fewer than half will relapse.
- After five years of sobriety, the chance of relapse is less than 15 percent.

During recovery, the brain can build new cues to not use drugs, in the same way it once built triggers to use them. For example, attending therapy and twelve-step meetings teaches people to call their sponsors (recovering addicts who commit to supporting other people in recovery) when cravings hit hard. The sponsor supports the recovering person in making the choice not to use. The choice to stay sober becomes a new reward and is itself a new trigger to stay sober. Sack says, "Over time the addict subconsciously dissociates the cue from the past reward of using [the drug] and associates it with the new reward of sobriety."

LIFE IN RECOVERY

Getting clean and staying sober is hard work. While it's easier for some people than others, most addicts find it to be one of the most difficult things they'll ever do. And the risk of relapse is always present, no matter how many years of sobriety. For example, Kimberly Bussey got clean after attending a six-month residential treatment program. She takes buprenorphine to maintain her sobriety. "The medication definitely helps. I don't want to say it's a cure-all. It takes a lot of internal, emotional work, along with the medication, to stay clean." She's been clean for seven years and wonders if she would be clean at all without the withdrawal medication.

Recovering addict Stephen Ahlert works hard to maintain his sobriety. "It's a constant battle with my addiction," he says, "but I fight every day and thank God that I'm winning the war, one day at a time." Everyday problems such as a lost job or a broken relationship may make the cravings for the abused drug nearly irresistible for an addict in recovery.

SAMHSA defines recovery as "a process of change through which individuals improve their health and wellness, live self-directed lives, and strive to reach their full potential." Most addicts did a lot of damage during their addiction—to themselves, to their family and friends, and to the communities where they live. Staying sober and using available resources can go a long way toward repairing that damage.

The Substance Abuse and Mental Health Services Administration describes the dimensions of recovery as

- **health**—overcoming or managing the addiction by abstaining from illicit drugs and nonprescribed medications, and by making informed, healthy choices that support physical and emotional well-being
- **home**—having a stable and safe place to live
- **purpose**—resuming meaningful daily activities, such as a job, school, seeing family and friends, and securing the independence, income, and resources to participate in society
- **community**—having relationships and social networks that provide support, friendship, love, and hope

Drug addicts in recovery exercise at a substance abuse treatment center in Westborough, Massachusetts. Exercise improves brain chemistry and overall general health. It also reduces stress and promotes self-confidence.

Recovering addicts may greatly benefit from the support and acceptance offered by continued attendance at twelve-step programs, periodic visits with counselors, or participation in faith-based activities. Some people do volunteer work, sharing their message of hope and recovery with others. Others mentor those in the early stages of recovery. It may take time for an addict in recovery to regain the trust and respect of family and friends, but it will happen. Hope is the catalyst for recovery, according to SAMHSA.

"If I could have chosen to stop using drugs I would have done so," says recovering heroin addict Alisha Choquette. "Being addicted to drugs steals so much from you. You are completely emotional and the ability to control your impulses, thoughts, and actions is nonexistent. Being a drug addict turned me into a totally different person than I otherwise would have been.

A rehab counselor high-fives an addict in recovery following a group therapy session at a substance abuse treatment center in Westborough, Massachusetts.

The absolute worst part of my addiction was the fact that it prevented me from being the best parent that I could have been; this has had a profound impact on my daughter's life." She adds, "Many may read my story and be disgusted by the fact that I used drugs while pregnant and 'chose' drugs over my child. The truth of the matter is I love my daughter more than anything in this entire world."

Choquette believes that "we can either use our experiences as a means to get down on ourselves and live in shame and regret, or we can use our experiences as a platform to reach better things in our life. I have chosen to use my negative experiences, to learn from them, and to use them to help others who are afflicted by this terrible disease of addiction."

Twenty-nine years old and drug-free, Choquette has a lot to feel good about in her life. She finished community college and is a licensed chemical dependency professional. She works as a substance abuse counselor at a residential drug treatment facility in Providence, Rhode Island. She also volunteers for Shine a Light on Heroin, a grassroots organization aimed at reducing the stigma associated with heroin addiction. Choquette shares her story with local high schools and hopes that one day she can open her own substance abuse treatment facility. "I'm finally comfortable in my own skin and am okay with the woman that I've become."

SOURCE NOTES

4   Donna Kull, interviews with author, February 28 to March 5, 2016.

4   Ibid.

4   Chuck Rosenberg, quoted in *2015 National Drug Threat Assessment Summary*, Drug Enforcement Administration, October 2015, http://www.dea.gov/docs/2015%20NDTA%20 Report.pdf.

4–5   Kull, interviews.

6   Ibid.

8   Donna Kull, January 13, 2016, comment on Adam Kull's Facebook page, https://www .facebook.com/adam.kull.10?fref=ts.

8   James Weinberg, January 25, 2016, comment on Adam Kull's Facebook page.

8   Brian Kull, interviews with author, February 28 to March 5, 2016.

8   Ibid.

10   Shoshana Herzig, quoted in "Researchers Identify Sharp Rise in Opioid-Related Hospitalizations, Health Care Costs," press release, *EurekAlert*! May 2, 2016, http://www .eurekalert.org/pub_releases/2016-05/bidm-ris042916.php.

13   Michele Leonhart, quoted in Barbara Goldberg, "A Legal Drug That's 50 Times More Powerful Than Heroin Blamed for an 'Alarming' Spike in Fatal Overdoses," *Business Insider*, March 19, 2015, http://www.businessinsider.com/r-powerful-opioid-fentanyl -blamed-for-spike-in-us-drug-overdoses-2015-3.

14   Ellen Hopkins, interview with author, April 8, 2016.

14   "What Is Addiction?," National Institute on Drug Abuse, accessed March 20, 2016, https:// easyread.drugabuse.gov/content/what-addiction.

14–15 Hopkins, interview.

15   Ibid.

15   Ibid.

15–16 Ibid.

16   Ibid.

20   William D. Stanley, quoted in Anna Swartz, "Why Are Opioids Addictive? The Science behind the Drugs," *Science.Mic*, February 19, 2016, http://mic.com/articles/135706 /why-are-opioids-addictive-the-science-behind-the-drugs#.GglOYUKoG.

22–23 Aaron Smith, quoted in "Breaking Point: Heroin in America," first broadcast March 11, 2016, on *20/20* by ABC, http://abc.go.com/shows/2020/episode-guide/2016-03/11 -031116-breaking-point-heroin-in-america.

23 Kimberly Bussey, quoted in Liz Szabo, "Advocates Push to Expand Use of Medications to Treat Addiction," *USA Today*, July 8, 2015, http://www.usatoday.com/story /news/2015/07/08/addiction-treatment-debate/29819285/.

23 Savanah (last name not given), quoted in "Breaking Point."

24 "Drug Facts: Understanding Drug Use and Addiction," National Institute on Drug Abuse, last modified August 2016, https://www.drugabuse.gov/publications/drugfacts /understanding-drug-abuse-addiction.

24 "What Is Addiction?," *Psychology Today*, accessed May 9, 2016, https://www .psychologytoday.com/basics/addiction.

26 Daniel J. Siegel, quoted in Michael Dahr, "Is the Teen Brain More Vulnerable to Addiction?," *Huffington Post*, January 21, 2014, http://www.huffingtonpost .com/2014/01/21/teen-brain-addiction-vulnerable_n_4638723.html.

27 Lucy, interview with author, March 23, 2016.

27 Nate, interview with author, March 2016.

28 Megan, interview with author, March 2016.

28–29 Alexandra, interview with author, March 2016.

30 Brian Kull, interviews with author.

31 Stephen Ahlert, interviews with author, May 2016.

31 Ibid.

31 Mark Nomady, quoted in Scott Glover, "Southern California Doctor Sentenced in Overdose Deaths of 3 Patients," *CNN*, February 5, 2016, http://www.cnn.com/2016/02/05/health /california-overdose-doctor-murder-sentencing/.

31–32 Ahlert, interviews.

32 Ibid.

32–33 Ibid.

33 Ibid.

33 Tom Frieden, quoted in Maggie Fox, "Drug Overdose Deaths Hit 'Alarming' New High in U.S., CDC Says," *NBC News*, December 18, 2015, http://www.nbcnews.com/health /health-news/drug-overdose-deaths-hit-new-record-u-s-cdc-says-n482746.

34 Susan Brink, "How Heroin Kills: What Might Have Happened to Philip Seymour Hoffman," *National Geographic*, February 4, 2014, http://news.nationalgeographic.com /news/2014/02/140204-philip-seymour-hoffman-actor-heroin-overdose/.

34 Andrew Kolodny, quoted in Tammie Smith, "Risks of Addiction with Prescription Opioids Underestimated," *Richmond Times-Dispatch,* October 23, 2015, http://www.richmond .com/life/health/article_705f0bb9-7341-59ad-acd5-6bf2d100c9cb.html.

34   Massimo Calabresi, quoted on cover, *Time* 185, no. 22 (June 15, 2015).

34–35   Massimo Calabresi, "Hooked: How Powerful Painkillers Created a National Epidemic," *Time* 185, no. 22 (June 15, 2015): 26–33.

35   Andrew Kolodny, quoted in Tony Leys, "Iowans Bought 300 Million Addictive Pills Last Year," *Des Moines Register,* February 28, 2016, http://www.desmoinesregister.com/story/news /health/2016/02/28/iowans-bought-300-million-addictive-pills-last-year/80990316/.

35   Ibid.

37   Tiffany Turner, quoted in Calabresi, "Hooked."

37   Andrew Kolodny, quoted in Katharine Q. Seelye, "Children of Heroin Crisis Find Refuge in Grandparents' Arms," *New York Times*, May 21, 2016, http://www.nytimes.com /interactive/2016/05/05/us/grandparents-heroin-impact-kids.html?_r=0.

38   Gina Kolata and Sarah Cohen, "Drug Overdoses Propel Rise in Mortality Rates of Young Whites," *New York Times*, January 16, 2016, http://www.nytimes.com/2016/01/17 /science/drug-overdoses-propel-rise-in-mortality-rates-of-young-whites.html?_r=0.

38   Andrew Kolodny, quoted in Allan Smith, "There's a Disturbing Theory about Why America's Overdose Epidemic Is Primarily Affecting White People," *Business Insider*, January 25, 2016, http://www.businessinsider.com/race-may-play-part-in-overdose -epidemic.

38   Jen Simon, "I'm a Stay-at-Home Mom. I'm an Addict," *Washington Post*, June 6, 2016, https://www.washingtonpost.com/news/parenting/wp/2016/06/06/im-a-stay-at-home -mom-im-an-addict/.

39   Editorial board, "Drug Deaths Reach White America," *New York Times*, January 25, 2016, http://www.nytimes.com/2016/01/25/opinion/drug-deaths-reach-white-america.html.

39–40   Sarah Gaskill, interviews with author, April 2016.

40   Ibid.

40   James Cross, quoted in Jon Collins, "He Sold Drugs to His Own Community; Now He Fights for Redemption," *MPR News*, April 18, 2016, http://www.mprnews.org /story/2016/04/18/opioid-profiles-james-cross.

42   Andrew Kolodny, quoted in Lisa Esposito, "Silent Epidemic: Seniors and Addiction," *U.S. News*, December 2, 2015, http://health.usnews.com/health-news/patient-advice /articles/2015/12/02/silent-epidemic-seniors-and-addiction.

42   Ibid.

42–43   Joseph Garbely, quoted in Esposito, "Silent Epidemic."

44   Judy Rummler, quoted in C. J. Arlotta, "How Prince's Death Can Help Abolish the Stigma of Opioid Addiction," *Forbes*, June 5, 2016, http://www.forbes.com/sites /cjarlotta/2016/06/05/how-princes-death-can-help-abolish-the-stigma-of-opioid -addiction/#328798c867b2.

48   Melanie Haiken, "Is the Super Potent New Opiate Painkiller Zohydro Just Too Dangerous?," *Forbes*, February 28, 2014, http://www.forbes.com/sites /melaniehaiken/2014/02/28/is-zohydro-the-super-potent-new-opiate-painkiller-just -too-dangerous/#4635fc511f68.

48   Andrew Kolodny, quoted in Haiken, "Super Potent."

49   Alex Lawson, "No Accident: Deadly Greed of Pharmaceutical Companies Drives the Heroin Epidemic," *Huffington Post*, January 20, 2016, http://www.huffingtonpost.com /alex-lawson/no-accident-deadly-greed_b_9031038.html.

50   Robert Califf, "Changing Course: A New Approach to Opioid Pain Medication at FDA," *FDA* (blog), February 5, 2016, http://blogs.fda.gov/fdavoice/index.php/2016/02/changing -course-a-new-approach-to-opioid-pain-medication-at-fda/.

51   Alisha Choquette, interviews with author, March and April, 2016.

51   L. Manchikanti and A. Singh, "Therapeutic Opioids: A Ten Year Perspective on the Complexities and Complications of the Escalating Use, Abuse, and Nonmedical Use of Opioids," *Pain Physician* 11, no. 2 (2008): S63–88, http://www.ncbi.nlm.nih.gov /pubmed/18443641.

51–52   Choquette, interviews.

52   Ibid.

52   Ibid.

53   Ibid.

53   Ibid.

53   Ibid.

54   Wilson Compton, quoted in Nicole Makris, "Prescription Drugs Are Leading to Heroin Addictions," Healthline, February 26, 2016, http://www.healthline.com/health-news /prescription-drugs-lead-to-addiction#1.

55–56   Ibid.

56   Rosenberg, quoted in *Drug Assessment Summary*.

57   Mark (no last name given), quoted in Susan Shultz, "Heroin: One Darien Story," *Darien* (CT) *Times*, February 25, 2016, http://www.darientimes.com/63745/heroin-one-darien -story/.

57   Ibid.

57–58   Michael (no last name given), quoted in Jason Smith, "Heroin in the Foothills, Part 1," *Auburn (CA) Journal*, July 17, 2014, http://www.auburnjournal.com/article/7/16/14 /heroin-foothills.

58   Ibid.

59   Tom Zimmerman, personal interview with author, May 2016.

59–60   Ibid.

60–61 Ibid.

61–62 Ibid.

62 Ibid.

62 Clorissa Jones, quoted in Duff Wilson and John Shiffman, "Newborns Die after Being Sent Home with Mothers Struggling to Kick Drug Addiction," *Reuters*, December 7, 2015, Getting Help video at 0:50, http://www.reuters.com/investigates/special-report/baby -opioids/#article-1-unprotected.

63 Earl Washburn, interview with author, January 19, 2016.

63–64 Ibid.

64 Ibid.

64 Leslie Kerzner, quoted in Lenny Bernstein, "When Life Begins in Rehab: A Baby Heals after a Mother's Heroin Addiction," *Washington Post*, August 12, 2015, https://www .washingtonpost.com/national/health-science/when-life-begins-in-rehab-a-maryland -baby-inherits-her-mothers-addiction/2015/08/12/182c8f50-37a4-11e5-9d0f -7865a67390ee_story.html.

64 Washburn, interview, January 19, 2016.

66 "AAPM Facts and Figures on Pain," American Academy of Pain Medicine, accessed February 5, 2016, http://www.painmed.org/patientcenter/facts_on_pain.aspx#refer.

67 Hsiu-Ying Tseng, quoted in Marisa Gerber, "Doctor Convicted of Murder for Patients' Drug Overdoses Gets 30 Years to Life in Prison," *LA Times*, February 5, 2016, http://www .latimes.com/local/lanow/la-me-ln-doctor-murder-overdose-drugs-sentencing -20160205-story.html.

68 Unnamed former patient, quoted in Katie Mettler, "Georgia's Alleged 'Dr. Death', Prescriber of Addictive Pain Medicines, Indicted on Three Counts of Murder after 36 of His Patients Die," *Washington Post*, May 19, 2016, https://www.washingtonpost.com /news/morning-mix/wp/2016/05/19/georgias-dr-death-prescriber-of-addictive-pain -medicines-indicted-on-three-counts-of-murder-after-36-of-his-patients-die/.

68 Tom Frieden, quoted in "CDC: Physicians Are Fueling Prescription Painkiller Overdoses," Robert Wood Johnson Foundation, July 2, 2014, http://www.rwjf.org/en/culture-of -health/2014/07/cdc_physicians_are.html.

69 Peter Staats, quoted in Gerber, "Doctor Convicted."

69 Earl R. Washburn, interviews with author, January and February 2016.

70 Ibid.

70 Lauren Kramer, interviews with author, January and February 2016.

70–71 Ibid.

71, 73 Robert Kingwell, interview with author, February 2016.

73 Ibid.

73 Ibid.

73   Bruce Psaty, quoted in Abby Goodnough and Sabrina Tavernise, "Opioid Prescriptions Drop for First Time in Two Decades," *New York Times*, May 20, 2016, http://www.nytimes .com/2016/05/21/health/opioid-prescriptions-drop-for-first-time-in-two-decades .html?_r=0.

74   "Opioid Painkiller Prescribing," CDC, July 2014, http://www.cdc.gov/vitalsigns/opioid -prescribing/.

74   CDC panel on opioid use, quoted in Lenny Bernstein, "CDC Urge Doctors to Curb Opioid Prescriptions: 'The Risks Are Addiction and Death, and the Benefits Are Unproven," *Washington Post*, December 14, 2015, https://www.washingtonpost.com/news /to-your-health/wp/2015/12/14/hoping-to-curb-the-prescription-opioid-epidemic-cdc -proposes-new-guidelines-for-doctors/.

74–75   Thomas Frieden, quoted in Liz Szabo, "Doctors Told to Avoid Prescribing Opiates for Chronic Pain," *USA Today*, March 16, 2016, http://www.usatoday.com/story /news/2016/03/15/cdc-issues-new-guidelines-opiate-prescribing-reduce-abuse -overdoses/81809704/.

75   Andrew Kolodny, quoted in Szabo, "Doctors Told to Avoid Prescribing Opiates."

76   Frieden, quoted in Szabo, "Doctors Told to Avoid Prescribing Opiates."

77   Chris Hansen, quoted in Szabo, "Doctors Told to Avoid Prescribing Opiates."

77   Kramer, interviews.

77   Ibid.

77–78   Robert Kingwell, interviews with author, January and February 2016.

78   Ibid.

78–79   Ibid.

80   Leeann Nielson, interviews with author, April and May 2016.

80   Adi Jaffe, quoted in Stuart Wolpert, "People Can Overcome Their Addictions, but Not Quickly, UCLA Psychologist Says," *UCLA Newsroom*, September 7, 2010, http://newsroom.ucla. edu/releases/people-can-overcome-their-addictions-170880.

80–81   Nielson, interviews.

81   Ibid.

82   Ibid.

82   Ibid.

82   Ibid.

83   Sarah Gaskill, interview with author, June 20, 2016.

83   James Cross, quoted in Collins, "He Sold Drugs."

83   *A Treatment Improvement Protocol: Improving Cultural Competence*, SAMHSA, 2014, accessed June 5, 2016. http://store.samhsa.gov/product/TIP-59-Improving-Cultural- Competence/SMA15-4849.

84   Jaffe, quoted in Wolpert, "People Can Overcome."

87   Gaskill, interview.

89   Jeffrey Allgaier, quoted in Molly Rosbach, "Opioids in Yakima: Medication Based Treatment Gains Traction," *Yakima (WA) Herald*, August 29, 2016, http://www .yakimaherald.com/lifestyle/health/opioids-in-yakima-medication-based-treatment -gains-traction/article_dbffe0f2-6ca1-11e6-987c-5f166635db5f.html.

91   William Hayes, quoted in Susan Svrluga, "The Drug Suboxone Could Combat the Heroin Epidemic. So Why Is It So Hard to Get?," *Washington Post*, January 13, 2015, https://www. washingtonpost.com/local/a-drug-called-suboxone-could-combat-the-heroin -epidemic-so-why-is-it-so-hard-to-get/2015/01/13/4135d08c-812e-11e4-9f38 -95a187e4c1f7_story.html.

92   Brian Shoichet, quoted in "Safer Opioid Painkiller Made from Scratch," *ScienceDaily*, August 17, 2016, https://www.sciencedaily.com/releases/2016/08/160817142554 .htm.

93   Tim Murphy, quoted in Szabo, "Advocates Push to Expand."

93–94 Dan Cain, "Experience Argues against Embrace of Medication-Assisted Treatment," *Addiction Professional*, August 15, 2013, http://www.addictionpro.com/article /experience-argues-against-embrace-medication-assisted-treatment?page=2.

94   Allgaier, quoted in Rosbach, "Opioids in Yakima."

95–96 Scott MacDonald, quoted in Andrew Duffy, "Vancouver Clinic Prescribes Medical-Grade Heroin to Chronic Addicts," *Ottawa (ONT) Citizen*, August 22, 2016, http://ottawacitizen .com/news/local-news/vancouver-clinic-prescribes-medical-grade-heroin-to-chronic -addicts.

96   Lynda LePretre, quoted in Duffy, "Vancouver Clinic."

96   Dave Napio, quoted in Dan Levin, "Vancouver Prescriptions for Addicts Gain Attention as Heroin and Opioid Use Rises," *New York Times*, April 21, 2016, http://www.nytimes .com/2016/04/22/world/americas/canada-vancouver-heroin-prescriptions.html?_r=0.

97   Randy Fincham, quoted in Levin, "Vancouver Prescriptions."

97–98 MacDonald, quoted in Levin, "Vancouver Prescriptions."

98   Ethan Nadelmann, editorial, "The War on Drugs," *Rolling Stone*, no. 1261 (May 19, 2016): 30.

98–99 MacDonald, quoted in Andrea Woo, "U.S. Senate Struggles with Concept of Prescription Heroin, Injection Sites," *Vancouver Globe and Mail*, June 15, 2016, http://www .theglobeandmail.com/news/british-columbia/us-senate-struggles-with-concept-of -prescription-heroin-injection-sites/article30482999/.

99   David Murray, quoted in Woo, "U.S. Senate."

100 David Sack, "Why Relapse Isn't a Sign of Failure," *Psychology Today* (blog), October 19, 2012, http://www.psychologytoday.com/blog/where-science-meets-the -steps/201210/why-relapse-isn't-a-sign-failure.

100–101 Ibid.

101   Ibid.

102   Bussey, quoted in Szabo, "Advocates Push to Expand."

102   Ahlert, interviews.

102   "Recovery and Recovery Support," SAMHSA, accessed June 15, 2016, http://www
      .samhsa.gov/recovery.

103–104 Choquette, interviews.

104   Ibid.

105   Ibid.

121   *Chasing Heroin*, film description, *Frontline*, February 23, 2016, http://www.pbs.or
      g/wgbh/frontline/film/chasing-heroin/.

GLOSSARY

abuse deterrent formulations: methods of manufacturing prescription painkillers to make it difficult or impossible to prepare them for snorting or injection. These recipes include time-release capsules and medications that melt into gels that cannot be injected.

addiction: a condition in which the repeated use of a drug that causes dependence leads to craving for the drug. The long-term use of the drug changes the brain chemistry and makes it extremely difficult to stop using the drug without experiencing painful withdrawal symptoms. People who are addicted to drugs generally continue to use even when doing so negatively impacts their lives, relationships, jobs, and health.

buprenorphine: a synthetic opioid medication (brand name Subutex) that reduces or eliminates opioid withdrawal symptoms and cravings by blocking opioid receptors in the brain. It comes in several forms including an implant that works for six months.

cocaine: a highly addictive drug made from the coca plant that users inject, snort, or inhale. Crack cocaine is a crystal form that is even more addictive than the powdered form.

computerized tomography (CT) scan: a series of computer-processed X-rays taken from different angles to create cross-sectional images of internal organs

culturally appropriate treatment: a model for addiction treatment that incorporates honor and respect for a person's traditions, philosophies, and behavior based on the person's age, gender, health, race, ethnicity, sexual orientation, or other identity

dependence: a condition in which a user must continue to take a drug, even a prescription painkiller, or face painful withdrawal symptoms

depressants: one of two general categories of drugs with potential for abuse. These drugs include prescription painkillers (such as OxyContin and Vicodin), prescription tranquilizers (such as Valium and Xanax), and heroin. These drugs relax the body by slowing the heart and breathing. If abused, any of these drugs can be lethal.

detoxification: clearing drugs out of the system. Also called detox, it may take five to seven days.

dopamine: a neurotransmitter produced in the brain that helps people focus and is responsible for drive and motivation. Dopamine is part of the brain's natural reward pathways. Addictive drugs trigger the release of more dopamine, and addicts crave the resulting high.

endorphin: a chemical substance produced in the brain that binds to opioid receptors and reduces pain and stress. It is one of the body's natural pain-relieving chemicals.

harm reduction programs: programs for addicts that focus on making drug use safer until the person is ready or able to quit using. Such programs include needle exchange, supervised injection sites, help with social services, and rehabilitation therapies for addicts who are not in treatment.

heroin: an illegal and highly addictive drug made from the opium poppy

medication-assisted treatment (MAT): a treatment for opioid drug addiction that can help ease withdrawal symptoms, decrease drug cravings, and dramatically cut the risk of relapse. The treatment relies on substituting one of various synthetic opioid substitutes for the addict's drug of choice. Over time, some people in MAT programs are able to get clean and do without the medications. Others may need to remain in MAT programs indefinitely.

methadone: a synthetic opioid medication most often used to treat heroin addiction. Methadone helps prevent withdrawal symptoms and reduces cravings by activating opioid receptors in the brain.

methamphetamine: an illegal and highly addictive synthetic stimulant. Methamphetamine is not an opioid or opiate, but abuse of the drug can cause overdose and death.

naloxone: when injected or sprayed into a nostril, this medication (brand name Narcan) reverses an opioid overdose almost immediately. Narcan "ejects" the opioid from the opioid receptors, essentially causing an instant withdrawal.

naltrexone: a medication (brand name Vivitrol) used to treat opioid addiction. It blocks the euphoria, cravings, and the sedative effects of opioids by binding to and blocking opioid receptors.

narcotic: a drug that relieves pain, dulls the senses, and promotes sleep. The term is most often used to describe legal opioid painkiller drugs such as OxyContin as well as illegal drugs such as heroin.

neonatal abstinence syndrome (NAS): the term doctors use for a baby born to a drug-addicted mother. The baby goes through withdrawal from the drug during its first days of life. Symptoms are severe and can include difficulty feeding, shaking, and seizures.

neuron: a nerve cell in the brain and body that transmits electrical and chemical messages

neurotransmitter: a chemical the brain produces to carry information between neurons in the brain. While information in the form of electrical impulses travels along the neurons, the electrical impulse cannot cross the gaps (synapses) between neurons. Some neurotransmitters calm the body, and others excite it.

opiate: a drug such as morphine, heroin, and codeine that comes directly from the opium poppy. Morphine and codeine have legitimate medical uses, mostly as painkillers. Heroin, however, is extremely addictive—much more so than morphine and codeine—and is illegal.

opioid: a synthetic medication that works in the brain like an opiate to relieve pain and anxiety. Opioids are highly addictive. They include brand name medications such as OxyContin and Vicodin.

opioid receptors: sites in the brain and spinal cord where natural endorphins and opioid drugs attach. When they attach, the brain releases dopamine, which relieves pain and stress and creates a strong feeling of well-being known as a high.

overdose: a dangerously large dose of a drug that may cause death if the user does not receive emergency medical care. Depressant drugs such as opioids slow down breathing and heart rate. Stimulant drugs such as methamphetamine speed up the heart and increase body temperature. Both types of drugs may lead to death by respiratory and cardiac arrest.

rehabilitation (rehab) program: a course of treatment that helps addicts overcome their addiction. Programs may be inpatient, where patients live in a facility such as a hospital or a residential center for a month or more. Day treatment programs require patients to come to a facility on a daily basis over a number of weeks. Other programs occur entirely on an outpatient basis. Rehab programs usually involve talk-therapy counseling, and many offer medication-assisted treatment.

reward pathways: a series of connections, or circuits, between areas of the brain that when triggered by endorphins lead to the perception of pleasure

stimulant: a type of drug (such as cocaine or methamphetamine) that excites a user's system by speeding up the heart and breathing

Suboxone: a brand name synthetic medication that combines buprenorphine and naloxone and is used to treat opioid addiction. The drug eases withdrawal symptoms, especially cravings.

synapse: a gap or space between two nerve cells in the brain. While information travels along nerves in the form of electrical impulses, these impulses cannot jump across the synapses. Instead, the brain makes chemicals called neurotransmitters that carry the information across the synapses.

tolerance: a condition in which the body gets used to a medication or drug such as prescription painkillers or heroin. The user must take increasingly large amounts of the drug to achieve the same effect or switch to another drug. Tolerance is often a factor in drug overdoses.

twelve-step programs: recovery programs, such as Alcoholics Anonymous (AA) and Narcotics Anonymous (NA), for people addicted to drugs, alcohol, and other unhealthy behaviors. The self-help programs rely on talk therapy in a group situation in which nonprofessionals encourage and support one another in their recovery. Meetings are available to adult and teen addicts, and separate twelve-step support groups are also available for families of addicts.

SELECTED BIBLIOGRAPHY ————————

Behavioral Health Trends in the United States: Results from the 2014 National Survey on Drug Use and Health. SAMHSA, September 2015. http://www.samhsa.gov/data/sites /default/files/NSDUH-FRR1-2014/NSDUH-FRR1-2014.pdf.

"Breaking Point: Heroin in America." First broadcast March 11, 2016, on *20/20* by ABC. http://abc.go.com/shows/2020/episode-guide/2016-03/11-031116-breaking-point -heroin-in-america.

Calabresi, Massimo. "Hooked: How Powerful Painkillers Created a National Epidemic." *Time* 185, no. 22 (June 15, 2015): 26–33.

"CDC Guideline for Prescribing Opioids for Chronic Pain—United States, 2016." *Centers for Disease Control and Prevention*. Last modified March 18, 2016. http://www.cdc.gov /mmwr/volumes/65/rr/rr6501e1.htm.

Collins, Jon. "He Sold Drugs to His Own Community; Now He Fights for Redemption." *MPR*, April 18, 2016. http://www.mprnews.org/story/2016/04/18/opioid-profiles -james-cross.

"Dramatic Increases in Maternal Opioid Use and Neonatal Abstinence Syndrome." National Institute on Drug Abuse. Last modified September 2015. https://www.drugabuse.gov /related-topics/trends-statistics/infographics/dramatic-increases-in-maternal-opioid -use-neonatal-abstinence-syndrome.

"Drug Facts: Understanding Drug Use and Addiction." National Institute on Drug Abuse. Last modified August 2016. https://www.drugabuse.gov/publications/drugfacts /understanding-drug-abuse-addiction.

"Drugs, Brains, and Behavior: The Science of Addiction." National Institute on Drug Abuse. Last modified July 2014. https://www.drugabuse.gov/publications/drugs-brains-behavior -science-addiction/preface.

Esposito, Lisa. "Silent Epidemic: Seniors and Addiction." *U.S. News*, December 2, 2015. http://health.usnews.com/health-news/patient-advice/articles/2015/12/02 /silent-epidemic-seniors-and-addiction.

Fox, Maggie. "Drug Overdose Deaths Hit 'Alarming' New High in US, CDC Says." *NBC News*, December 18, 2015. http://www.nbcnews.com/health/health-news/drug-overdose -deaths-hit-new-record-u-s-cdc-says-n482746.

Gerber, Marisa. "Doctor Convicted of Murder for Patients' Drug Overdoses Gets 30 Years to Life in Prison," *LA Times*, February 5, 2016. http://www.latimes.com/local/lanow/la-me-ln -doctor-murder-overdose-drugs-sentencing-20160205-story.html.

Goodman, Jack. "One Man's Journey out of Addiction to Pain Killers." *New York City Lens*, February 11, 2016. http://nycitylens.com/2016/02/one-mans-journey-out-of -addiction-to-pain-killers/.

"Increases in Drug and Opioid Overdose Deaths—United States, 2000–2014." Centers for Disease Control and Prevention, January 1, 2016. http://www.cdc.gov/mmwr/preview /mmwrhtml/mm6450a3.htm?dom=pscau&src=syn.

Kolata, Gina, and Sarah Cohen. "Drug Overdoses Propel Rise in Mortality Rates of Young Whites." *New York Times*, January 16, 2016. http://www.nytimes.com/2016/01/17 /science/drug-overdoses-propel-rise-in-mortality-rates-of-young-whites.html?_r=0.

Levin, Dan. "Vancouver Prescriptions for Addicts Gain Attention as Heroin and Opioid Use Rises." *New York Times*, April 21, 2016. http://www.nytimes.com/2016/04/22/world /americas/canada-vancouver-heroin-prescriptions.html?_r=0.

"Medication Assisted Treatment for Substance Abuse Disorders." SAMHSA, July 11, 2014. http://www.samhsa.gov/sites/default/files/topics/behavioral_health/medication -assisted-treatment-joint-bulletin.pdf.

"National Helpline." SAMHSA. Last modified September 11, 2014. http://www.samhsa.gov /find-help/national-helpline.

"Opioid Overdose. "Understanding the Epidemic." Centers for Disease Control and Prevention. Last modified June 21, 2016. http://www.cdc.gov/drugoverdose/epidemic/index.html.

"Opioid Painkiller Prescribing." Centers for Disease Control and Prevention, July 2014. http://www.cdc.gov/vitalsigns/opioid-prescribing/.

Sack, David. "Why Relapse Isn't a Sign of Failure." *Psychology Today* (blog). October 19, 2012. https://www.psychologytoday.com/blog/where-science-meets-the -steps/201210/why-relapse-isnt-sign-failure.

Seelye, Katharine. "Children of Heroin Crisis Find Refuge in Grandparents' Arms." *New York Times*, May 21, 2016. http://www.nytimes.com/interactive/2016/05/05/us /grandparents-heroin-impact-kids.html?_r=0.

Shultz, Susan. "Heroin: One Darien Story." *Darien (CT) Times*, February 25, 2016. http://www.darientimes.com/63745/heroin-one-darien-story/.

Smith, Allan. "There's a Disturbing Theory about Why America's Overdose Epidemic Is Primarily Affecting White People." *Business Insider*, January 25, 2016. http://www.businessinsider.com/race-may-play-part-in-overdose-epidemic.

Smith, Jason. "Heroin in the Foothills, Part 1." *Auburn (CA) Journal*, July 17, 2014. http://www .auburnjournal.com/article/7/16/14/heroin-foothills.

Szabo, Liz. "Advocates Push to Expand Use of Medications to Treat Addiction." *USA Today*, July 8, 2015. http://www.usatoday.com/story/news/2015/07/08/addiction-treatment -debate/29819285/.

———. "Doctors Told to Avoid Prescribing Opiates for Chronic Pain." *USA Today*, March 18, 2016. http://www.usatoday.com/story/news/2016/03/15/cdc-issues-new-guidelines -opiate-prescribing-reduce-abuse-overdoses/81809704/.

"A Treatment Improvement Protocol: Improving Cultural Competence." SAMHSA. Accessed June 5, 2016. http://store.samhsa.gov/product/TIP-59-Improving-Cultural-Competence /SMA15-4849.

2015 National Drug Threat Assessment Summary. Drug Enforcement Administration, October 2015. http://www.dea.gov/docs/2015%20NDTA%20Report.pdf.

Werthein, L. Jon. "Smack Epidemic: How Painkillers Are Turning Young Athletes into Heroin Addicts." *Sports Illustrated*. 122, no. 25 (June 22, 2015): 66–71.

"What Science Tells Us about Opioid Abuse and Addiction." National Institute on Drug Abuse, January 27, 2016. https://www.drugabuse.gov/about-nida/legislative-activities /testimony-to-congress/2016/what-science-tells-us-about-opioid-abuse-addiction.

FURTHER INFORMATION

BOOKS

Gammill, Joani. *Painkillers, Heroin, and the Road to Sanity: Real Solutions for Long-Term Recovery from Opiate Addiction*. Center City, MN: Hazelden, 2014. This registered nurse, author, and recovering addict specializes in drug and alcohol interventions. She has appeared on television shows and offers new hope and methods for recovery for addicts and for those who have relapsed.

Goldsmith, Connie. *Understanding Suicide: A National Epidemic*. Minneapolis: Twenty-First Century Books, 2017. Read more about the link between mental health conditions, suicide, substance abuse, and overdose. One-third of people who die by suicide are under the influence of alcohol or drugs at the time of their death.

Goldstein, Margaret J. *Legalizing Marijuana: Promises and Pitfalls*. Minneapolis: Twenty-First Century Books, 2017. Medical marijuana use, mostly for relief of chronic pain, is currently legal in twenty states and the District of Columbia. Recreational and medical use of marijuana is currently allowed in eight states. Learn about the movement to legalize marijuana and what it means for patients, state economies, and legal systems, and how it contributes to the national conversation about drug use and addiction.

Hopkins, Ellen. *Crank Trilogy*. New York: Margaret K. McElderry Books, 2013. These three books—*Crank*, *Glass*, and *Fallout*—tell the story of a young addict called Kristina and her addiction to methamphetamine. Kristina's addiction shatters her life and the lives of her family and children. Told in the author's award-winning free verse and based on the true story of the author's daughter, the books provide an eye-opening window into the world of drug addiction.

Jones, Patrick. *Teen Incarceration: From Cell Bars to Ankle Bracelets*. Minneapolis: Twenty-First Century Books, 2017. Many American teens end up in the juvenile justice system as a result of drug addiction. The system has moved away from harsh punishment and toward alternative models that include education, skill building, and therapy. Meet teens who have been in the system and learn more about alternative models of treatment and restorative justice.

Lembke, MD, Anna. *Drug Dealer, MD: How Doctors Were Duped, Patients Got Hooked, and Why It's So Hard to Stop*. Baltimore: Johns Hopkins University Press, 2016. Stanford psychiatrist and addiction researcher Dr. Anna Lembke explores the many factors behind the opioid epidemic in the United States. She discusses the need for more physician training and stresses her belief that pharmaceutical companies are part of the problem, exercising too much influence on health-care policy and decision making.

Lew, Kristi. *The Truth about Oxycodone and Other Narcotics*. New York: Rosen, 2014. This book for teen readers focuses on prescription opioid medications, how they affect the brain, how addiction happens, and strategies for recovery. It also offers tips on how to avoid addiction before it even starts.

Myers, Walter Dean. *Dope Sick*. New York: Amistad, 2009. Lil J, a seventeen-year-old inner city boy, is in big trouble. He holes up in an abandoned building as police chase him after a drug deal gone bad. Lil J steals pills from his mom and is developing a heroin habit. He meets a man named Kelly who challenges him to make changes that will avoid his predestined outcome of suicide.

Narcotics Anonymous Fellowship. *Living Clean: The Journey Continues*. Van Nuys, CA: Narcotics Anonymous, 2012. This book, written and published by NA, can be used at any stage of recovery, whether it's an addict's first try at recovery or whether NA has been guiding recovery for many years. It's relevant for both newcomers and to help experienced members develop an understanding of personal transformation.

Nolan, Han. *Born Blue*. San Diego: Harcourt Children's Books, 2001. This classic best-selling novel tells the story of Janie, the barely surviving daughter of a heroin addict. She's seen it all, including foster homes, physical abuse, and an unwanted pregnancy. She's determined to make a new life for herself and turns to her innate talent—singing—the only thing that makes her feel whole.

FILMS

Cake. Directed by Daniel Barnz. 102:00. Beverly Hills, CA: Twentieth Century Fox Home Entertainment, 2014. Nominated for Golden Globe Awards (best actress and best drama) and for a Screen Actors Guild Award for best actress (Jennifer Aniston), this film follows a young woman with chronic pain whose addiction to alcohol and prescription painkillers is wrecking her life.

Chasing Heroin. 114:00. *Frontline*, February 23, 2016. http://www.pbs.org/wgbh/frontline/film/chasing-heroin/. "A searing, two-hour investigation places America's heroin crisis in a fresh and provocative light—telling the stories of individual addicts, but also illuminating the epidemic's years-in-the-making social context . . . examining shifts in U.S. drug policy, and exploring what happens when addiction is treated like a public health issue, not a crime."

Chasing the Dragon: The Life of an Opiate Addict. US Drug Enforcement Agency and the Federal Bureau of Investigation. 49:08. Quantico, VA: FBI TV Studios, 2016. https://www.fbi.gov/news/stories/raising-awareness-of-opioid-addiction. This documentary film profiles Americans who have abused opiates. It looks at the cycle of addiction and the consequences associated with opioid abuse. Doctors and law enforcement officials discuss how the epidemic is unlike any the United States has seen before.

The Reward Pathway Reinforces Behavior. Genetic Science Learning Center, University of Utah. Accessed September 3, 2016. http://learn.genetics.utah.edu/content/addiction/rewardbehavior/. This narrated interactive slide show demonstrates how reward pathways work inside the human brain through ten animated slides.

WEBSITES

Centers for Disease Control and Prevention (CDC)
> 1600 Clifton Road
> Atlanta, GA 30329-4027
> (800) 232-4636
> http://www.cdc.gov
> Among other functions, this US government agency tackles the biggest health problems causing death and disability for Americans. These problems include addiction and overdose. The website section on Persons Who Use Drugs (http://www.cdc.gov/pwud/) provides extensive information about drugs, addiction, and treatment. The section on opioid overdose (http://www.cdc.gov/drugoverdose/data/) contains extensive data and statistics about the current opioid abuse and overdose epidemic.

Narcotics Anonymous (NA)
> PO Box 9999
> Van Nuys, CA 91409
> (818) 773-9999
> https://www.na.org/
> http://www.nar-anon.org/narateen/
> NA members hold more than sixty-three thousand meetings weekly in 132 countries. The group offers recovery from addiction with its twelve-step program. Regular attendance at group meetings is encouraged because a group atmosphere provides peer support and a network for addicts who are committed to pursue and maintain a life free of drugs. Narateen offers group support for teens with an addicted friend or family member.

National Institute on Drug Abuse (NIDA)
> Office of Science Policy and Communications, Public Information and Liaison Branch
> 6001 Executive Boulevard
> Room 5213, MSC 9561
> Bethesda, MD 20892-9561
> (301) 443-1124
> https://www.drugabuse.gov/
> https://teens.drugabuse.gov/ (for teens)
> A division of the National Institutes of Health, this US government research organization is a premier source of addiction facts and statistics, aiming to change the course of addiction treatment in the United States. The teen site was created for middle and high school students and their teachers to provide accurate and timely information for use in and out of the classroom.

Rehab International: Drug and Alcohol Rehab Guides
(877) 345-3281 (staffed 24-7)
http://rehab-international.org/
This site provides information on the most often abused drugs, treatment options in all states, how addiction develops and progresses, how to choose a treatment plan, and what to expect from treatment.

Substance Abuse and Mental Health Services Administration (SAMHSA)
5600 Fishers Lane
Rockville, MD 20857
(877) 726-4727
http://www.samhsa.gov/
This government-sponsored organization is a branch of the US Department of Health and Human Services. SAMHSA specializes in research on drug addiction, treatment, and recovery. The site provides detailed information about opioids and other drugs of addiction, substance abuse, recovery strategies, and mental health issues.

INDEX

PHOTO ACKNOWLEDGMENTS

The images in this book are used with the permission of: © Laura Westlund (charts throughout); backgrounds: © iStockphoto.com/Vladimirovic; © iStockphoto.com/EHStock; © ImageFlow/Shutterstock.com; © iStockphoto.com/nuiiun (syringe); © iStockphoto.com/wragg, p. 3; Courtesy of Brian and Donna Kull, p. 5; © Steve Granitz/Wire Image/Getty Images, p. 6; © Larry D. Moore/Wikimedia Commons (CC SA 3.0), p. 15; © Jinrikisha Amufabalo/Wikimedia Commons (CCO 1.0), p. 21; © Tetra Images/Alamy, p. 27; © pixelfit/E+/Getty Images, p. 32; © Hero Images/Getty Images, p. 35; © Kyndell Harkness/Minneapolis Star Tribune/ZUMA Press, p. 41; © Frank Micelotta/Getty Images, p. 43; © Derek Davis/Portland Press Herald, p. 45; © Alisha Choquette, p. 52; © Hero Images/Getty Images, p. 54; © Jim Cummins/The Image Bank/Getty Images, p. 59; © iStockphoto.com/vencavolrab , p. 60; © Andersen Ross/DigitalVision/Getty Images, p. 62; © Irfan Khan/Los Angeles Times/Getty Images, p. 67; © iStockphoto.com/Staras , p. 71; © Dean Hanson/Albuquerque Journal/ZUMA Press, p. 72; © Mira/Alamy, p. 81; © Steve Debenport/Getty Images, p. 87; Greg Gilbert/The Seattle Times., p. 91; © Jeff Vinnick/Getty Images, p. 96; © John Moore/Getty Images, pp. 103, 104.

Front cover: GIPhotoStock/Getty Images.

Jacket flaps: © iStockphoto.com/Vladimirovic.

Back cover: © iStockphoto.com/backpack555.

ABOUT THE AUTHOR

Connie Goldsmith has written nineteen nonfiction books for middle grade and young adult readers and has also published more than two hundred magazine articles for adults and children. Her recent YA nonfiction books include *Dogs at War: Military Canine Heroes; Understanding Suicide: A National Epidemic; The Ebola Epidemic: The Fight, The Future* (a Junior Library Guild selection); and *Bombs over Bikini: The World's First Nuclear Disaster,* also a Junior Library Guild Selection, a Children's Book Committee at Bank Street College Best Children's Book of the Year, and an SCBWI Crystal Kite winner.

Goldsmith is an active member of the Society of Children's Book Writers and Illustrators and a member of the Authors Guild. She is a registered nurse with a bachelor of science degree in nursing and a master of public administration degree in health care. When she's not writing, she visits with friends and family, pounds out the miles on her treadmill, plays with her crazy cats, and hikes along the American River near Sacramento, California, where she lives.